Grover Cleveland

22nd and 24th President of the United States

Grover Cleveland

22nd and 24th President of the United States

David R. Collins

 GARRETT EDUCATIONAL CORPORATION

Copyright © 1988 by David R. Collins

Manufactured in the United States of America

Edited and produced by Synthegraphics Corporation

Library of Congress Cataloging in Publication Data

Collins, David R.
  Grover Cleveland: 22nd and 24th President of the United States.

  (Presidents of the United States)
  Bibliography: p.
  Includes index.
  Summary: Follows the life of Grover Cleveland from birth to death, including his childhood, education, employment, and political career.
  1. Cleveland, Grover, 1837–1908 – Juvenile literature. 2. Presidents – United States – Biography – Juvenile literature. [1. Cleveland, Grover, 1837–1908. 2. Presidents]
  I. Title.
E697.C65 1988   973.8′5′0924 [B] [92]   87-35794
  ISBN 0-944483-01-1

_10.88_

Contents

Chronology for
Grover Cleveland

1837   Born on March 18

1841   Moved with family to Fayetteville, New York

1850   Moved with family to Clinton, New York; studied at Clinton Academy

1854   Moved to Buffalo, New York; began studying law

1859   Admitted to the bar by New York State Supreme Court

1862   Appointed assistant district attorney

1870   Elected sheriff of Erie County

1881   Elected mayor of Buffalo

1882   Elected governor of New York

1884   Elected 22nd President of the United States

1886   Married Frances Folsom on June 2

1888   Defeated for re-election by Benjamin Harrison

1889   Moved to New York City to practice law

1892   Elected 24th President of the United States

1897   Moved to Princeton, New Jersey

1908   Died on June 24

This photograph of Grover Cleveland was taken in the summer of 1888. He had completed his first term in office and was picked by the Democratic Party to run for a second term. (Library of Congress.)

Chapter 1

The Great Cover-up

If ever there was a night in American history cloaked in mystery and intrigue, it was the night of June 30, 1893. The setting was a yacht resting in the water off Pier A in New York City's East River. Since late afternoon, an unusual collection of passengers had boarded the *Oneida*, a luxurious yacht owned by E. C. Benedict. The wealthy Benedict entertained frequently, and among his friends and acquaintances were many of the country's social and financial elite. He was also known to be a close friend and firm supporter of President Grover Cleveland. Therefore, it was not a major surprise when the heavyset chief executive made his appearance aboard the *Oneida*.

Perhaps Cleveland hoped to enjoy a brief cruise before returning to the staggering demands of his office. The President looked unusually tired, his skin pale and a bit puffy, his thick moustache somewhat disheveled. An astute observer might also think it a trifle strange that Cleveland would be traveling without his wife Frances. The couple seldom vacationed apart since their White House wedding seven years earlier.

Indeed, the majority of the guests aboard the *Oneida* were medical men. Summoned to a mission wrapped in secrecy, these men were about to take part in a historic drama that many would label the greatest executive cover-up that ever took place.

TREATMENT FOR THE PRESIDENT AND THE ECONOMY

At the center of the cover-up was the President himself, who was then in the fourth month of his second presidency. He had served a previous term, from 1885–1889, only to be defeated in a bid for re-election by Republican Benjamin Harrison. Four years later, however, Cleveland was swept back into office. He immediately faced grave economic problems that threatened the financial stability of the United States government.

Gold vs. Silver

The crux of the economic problems was the unbalanced value of gold and silver, both of which were used for U.S. currency. The gold dollar carried a full value of 100 cents, with the federal gold reserve $3 million below the limit set by Congress. On the other hand, the silver dollar rested at a value of between 50 and 55 cents. Not only was a surplus of silver being mined in the United States, the market was glutted by imports from Europe and India. The reason silver was mined so aggressively and imported from abroad was the Sherman Silver Purchase Act. This act, which was passed by Congress in 1890, required the United States government to pay for silver as if it was still worth 100 cents on the dollar.

Cleveland's financial advisors were more and more convinced the nation might become bankrupt if it continued paying one dollar for 50 cents worth of silver. But only Congress could change the Sherman Act, and Congress had adjourned for the summer. Feeling that the matter was urgent, Cleveland ordered the lawmakers back into session on August 7. He only hoped he would live long enough to see the Sherman Silver Purchase Act repealed.

On the same day Cleveland announced the August date

for reconvening Congress, he slipped out of Washington and headed for Benedict's yacht. Only a handful of people knew the President's actual plans for the next five weeks, from June 30 until August 7. Cleveland felt it was imperative that the public not know that their chief executive was a very sick man.

Medical Opinions

It had all started with a sore spot on the roof of Cleveland's mouth. Never one to pamper himself, he ignored the problem until the pain became constant. During an examination by White House physician R. M. O'Reilly, a small portion of the diseased tissue was removed and sent to the Army Medical Museum for examination. An analysis revealed that a cancerous ulcer was alive and growing in the President's mouth. Surgery was recommended, the sooner the better.

"Can you get it all if you operate?" Cleveland wanted to know. "We won't know until we go in," came the answer. Cleveland's personal doctor, Joseph D. Bryant, agreed that surgery was needed.

Just as the physicians were convinced an operation was necessary, Cleveland was equally certain that secrecy was demanded. At 56, the President had always presented himself to be hearty and healthy. There was no hiding the fact that he was considerably overweight, yet the extra pounds seemed almost to add to his image, giving him an appearance of power and strength.

Although the country was at peace, Cleveland found a myriad of troubles waiting for him when he took office on March 4, 1893. Most of the problems were financial, requiring careful and cautious action. In Cleveland's mind, little would be gained and a great deal lost if the public suspected that not only the economy, but their elected leader was seriously ill. It was for this reason that President Grover Cleveland joined a small circle of medical men and a small crew aboard the *Oneida* that fateful evening in June of 1893. To the public, the President was simply going to enjoy a leisurely cruise with a few friends, eventually joining his wife and daughter at Sippican Harbor in Massachusetts.

The Secret Operation

The living room of the *Oneida* became an operating room for a dentist and five doctors. Following a thorough examination on the morning of July 1, Cleveland was deemed physically able to withstand the cancer surgery. After the dentist extracted two teeth, Dr. Bryant proceeded with the operation. Because the cancerous ulcer proved to be deeper and larger than was originally thought, the entire left upper jaw had to be removed. The cavity was stuffed so the cheek would appear normal and the President's words could be understood. By July 3, Cleveland was walking and taking liquid nourishment.

When the *Oneida* reached Sippican Harbor on July 5, a large group of reporters was waiting. One of Cleveland's aides turned aside their questions and requests to see the President by explaining that he was suffering from rheumatism. However, when word got around that it was something more serious, possibly cancer, the newsmen were even more insistent. Cleveland's old friend, Secretary of State Daniel Lamont, gave them a lecture about the importance of responsible journalism. He then told the reporters that the President also had needed some dental work done and took care of it while on the cruise. This was hardly headline news, so most of the reporters pursued it no further.

Unfortunately, the initial operation failed to remove all the cancerous tissue. When Dr. Bryant discovered this, the medical team was again summoned aboard the *Oneida* and traveled to Massachusetts. Once more the President boarded the craft, claiming he was embarking on a brief sailing expedition. Taking extra time and care, Dr. Bryant removed all tissue bearing the slightest signs of cancer.

Once his strength returned, Cleveland headed back to Gray Gables, the family vacation cottage. Although the doctors were confident they had taken out all the deadly cancer, Cleveland was not as convinced. Often he felt he was going to die. Yet he maintained an outer composure that hid his inner thoughts. Although the surgery had been performed through the mouth, there were no obvious signs of what had happened. Credit for masking the effect of the surgery went to one of Cleveland's doctors, who managed to put together a vulcanized rubber jaw that filled out the cheek and allowed the President to speak clearly.

CRISIS IN CONGRESS

By the first week in August, Cleveland was beginning to feel like his former robust self. He knew he would have to speak to Congress with force and effectiveness if he hoped to win repeal of the Sherman Silver Purchase Act. Legislators from the mining states would want the government to keep buying great amounts of silver regardless of the consequences. They had an eloquent spokesman for their cause in Congressman William Jennings Bryan of Nebraska. Bryan had supported Cleveland in past campaigns, but the bitter dispute over gold and silver values had brought about a major rift between the two men. (Bryan would win the next Democratic presidential nomination in 1896.)

Returning to the reconvened Congress, representatives and senators carried with them the mood of the moment across the nation—and it was not a cheerful one. Money, whether it be paper, gold, or silver, was in short supply and rumors spread everywhere about possible bank closings. Industrial workers blamed employers for the country's bleak financial condition, while the employers pointed their fingers at government leaders. Midwest farmers complained of low prices for crops and blamed millionaires in the East who knew little about agriculture and nothing about sacrifice.

Fear and nervousness had found their way into urban and rural homes, causing conflict and bickering among the closest of families. "I do not pretend to understand the nation's economy," wrote one Iowa farmer to Cleveland, "but I do know I will soon lose my wife and my homestead if something is not done to solve the existing problems. I wish I could help you, but your difficulties are beyond my knowledge so I can only send you my prayers." Such sentiments were typical among Americans in August of 1893 – people sensed the confusion of economic uncertainty, yet could do little to provide a cure.

Although Cleveland did not claim to have an instant solution to the depression, he insisted he knew where to start: the Sherman Silver Purchase Act had to be repealed. His message to Congress was logical and calm, and he made clear the urgent need to act. Weakened by the physical ordeal of the past weeks and drained by the heat in summertime Washington, Cleveland then retreated to Massachusetts while the Congressmen debated the issue.

The House and Senate Fight

Carrying the banner for the pro-silver forces was Congressman Bryan, who entranced his colleagues with a three-hour speech given without notes and filled with facts. His voice rose and fell, shouted and trembled, as he presented his arguments in behalf of silver coinage and a silver standard. Others also rose to speak in behalf of maintaining the Sherman Act, but no one could approach the powerful oratory of Bryan.

For three weeks the members of the House of Representatives debated what action to follow. When a vote was finally taken on August 28, the Sherman Silver Purchase Act was repealed by a vote of 239 to 108. Cleveland had crossed the first hurdle.

The issue took on a personal significance when it reached the Senate. Several senators from the western United States not only had close ties with the silver mining industry, they owned mines themselves. "The fight will become even rougher in the Senate," Cleveland observed to his advisors, "because we are suggesting taking money out of the pockets of some of the men who sit there." The President was right, and before the debate was finished many long-lasting friendships in the Senate had been broken.

Although outnumbered, the pro-silver senators formed an unusually tight-knit group. They fought with an intensity seldom witnessed, and Cleveland was maligned more than once by Democratic companions who had previously worked hard in his campaigns.

Into October the discussion continued, with those favoring silver coinage and the Sherman Act desperately seeking some form of compromise. At one point there seemed to be a chance that some give and take might be possible. But one man refused to budge from his original position opposing the Sherman Silver Purchase Act. "This government cannot continue unless silver purchases cease," Cleveland stated emphatically. "The House of Representatives has acted and now the Senate must take similar action." When the vote came on October 30, the senators followed Cleveland's directive by a 48 to 37 margin.

A Sad Victory

The internal fighting within the Democratic Party had been deep and personal. Still attempting to regain the physical strength drained by the cancer operations, Cleveland took little joy from the legislative victory. Indeed, the money standard was but one of many economic problems facing the nation in 1893.

Although Cleveland was convinced that his support of the gold standard was correct, he knew the prolonged squabbling in both the House and Senate had caused considerable damage. Unlike most congressional arguments, which are political, Democrats against Republicans, this one had transcended party lines. In doing so, it had left personal scars among individuals who once had worked closely with each other. Pulling the leadership of the nation together into a unified team would be a tremendous challenge for the President.

"There are times when I long for the carefree days of my youth growing up along the Erie Canal," Cleveland wrote to a friend in November of 1893. "Or the cheerful nights with my friends in Buffalo. But the portals of those days are closed forever and cannot be opened except in memory. . ."

It was not surprising that Cleveland would have found pleasure in looking back on his life, for few men in American history climbed the ladder of political prominence as swiftly as he did. In 1880, he was simply one of several successful practicing attorneys in Buffalo, New York. Five years later found him taking the oath of office as the 22nd President of the United States. There are those who might declare that the story of Grover Cleveland could "only happen in America." They could be right.

Chapter 2

Pranks and Prayers

"There's little joy bein' a middlin' boy." That was a favorite saying among large families in America during the 19th century. It called attention to the fact that while the older members of a family were given special privileges due to their age, and younger members were often spoiled because of their cuteness, children falling in the middle were often merely overlooked.

Stephen Grover Cleveland posed just such a potential problem. Born March 13, 1837, in Caldwell, New Jersey, he was welcomed by four older brothers and sisters. In the immediate years that followed, four more children were born to the Cleveland family. As long as Reverend Richard Cleveland had the means to feed and clothe his offspring, he declared proudly from the church pulpit that "it was God's noble purpose to share the gift of life to himself and his wife Ann."

Obedient to her husband's declaration, Ann Neal Cleveland nonetheless had ideas of her own. Raised in a southern society of colorful hooped skirts, grand plantations, and house servants, she saw nothing wrong with enjoying the fun and challenges of this world while preparing for heavenly rewards in the next. "So you must use all your resources," she told her nine children. "The Lord helps them who help themselves."

This imposing home in Caldwell, New Jersey, was the birthplace of Grover Cleveland, the only man to serve two non-sequential terms as President. (Library of Congress.)

A BOY–AND MAN–OF DISTINCTION

No one heard the advice more clearly than young Stephen Grover. As soon as he could, he dropped the first name, Stephen, and began using Grover. "It's more distinctive," he noted for those who inquired. "I'd like to make something of myself in this world and I think it will help if I have a name people will remember."

It was a harmless notion and most people merely chuckled at the young boy's seriousness about his future. Since his parents had selected the name Stephen to honor a deceased minister in Caldwell, and not a relative, they did not challenge their son's decision to change his name.

In a New Setting

After the Cleveland family moved to Fayetteville, New York, in 1841, Grover had many opportunities to test his own resourcefulness. In the town of 1,000, there was always a fence to paint or a carriage to clean. Once his own family chores were finished, the boy went door-to-door looking for extra tasks. It was well known in the town that Reverend Cleveland collected a yearly salary of $600. But even though the minister and his family were given a 2½-story frame house free to live in, pennies could only stretch so far in such a large family.

Grover was hired often by the townspeople to do odd jobs, and he showed his appreciation by completing a task as quickly and professionally as a boy could. Hailing bargemen on the Erie Canal to stop for a load of limestone was always good for a dime from the owners of the local quarries. Grover would often get up in the middle of the night so he would be the first boy on the job. After all, 10 cents could buy a juicy slice of meat for supper or two dozen eggs for breakfast.

Young Grover also proved himself an able student in the

one-room Fayetteville schoolhouse. Only rarely did he feel
the sting of the birch rod kept beside the schoolmaster's desk
to be used for pupil laziness or misbehavior. It was not so
much the physical pain that accompanied the switching that
bothered Grover. Being big-boned and rather fat, he suffered
little from the occasional punishment he received at school.
Rather, it was the lecture he received from his father afterwards that the boy hated most. It was difficult to understand
how failure to memorize a multiplication table was a direct
insult against God. But Reverend Cleveland made it seem so,
and his lectures were always long and agonizing.

A Brief Rebellion

There is little doubt that being "a minister's kid" put much
strain on young Grover Cleveland. Fayetteville was too small
a town for families not to be noticed and talked about—and
no one was more frequently evaluated than the offspring of
religious leaders.

Sundays were especially stressful for Grover because it
meant sitting through two lengthy church services and cate-
chism recitations as well. Reverend Cleveland urged a full
day of worship service, public and private, with every extra
moment spent in silent prayer. It was not a time for merri-
ment and fun, but rather an opportunity for solitude and reflec-
tion, for evaluating the past week in the eyes of a good
Christian. For a lively Grover Cleveland, every Sunday was
sheer torture. It was on just such a Sunday night that the boy
received an invitation he could not refuse.

"We're goin' ring the schoolhouse bell at midnight," a
friend told Grover. "Do you wanna come?"

Grover's face brightened with just the thought of such
a daring deed. "You bet I do!"

All the plans to get into the schoolhouse worked
perfectly. Promptly at midnight the loud bell tolled. The men
and women of Fayetteville scrambled into their clothes and

ran from their homes to see what was happening. Sadly, though, the three young bellringers had planned everything except their escape. Somehow they managed to lock themselves inside the empty schoolhouse, only to be brought out and escorted home by their disgruntled parents. The bell-ringing incident was retold time and again by the people of Fayetteville, but Grover seldom later mentioned the prank.

An Education Incomplete

Reverend Richard Cleveland was a graduate of Yale. And although a minister's salary did not go far in raising nine children, it was always understood that the Cleveland sons would receive the best formal education possible. (Women at that time seldom went to college.)

When Grover was 11, he was taken out of the one-room school in Fayetteville and enrolled in a local private academy with a pre-college curriculum. Two years later, in 1850, Reverend Cleveland accepted the position as director of the American Home Missionary Society in Clinton, New York. It meant moving the family, but because the new job doubled the minister's salary, it was an opportunity he could not refuse. For a brief time Grover attended Clinton Academy, but when financial problems continued to trouble the family, he returned to Fayetteville in 1852 to work in a general store.

It was not an easy life for a 15-year-old boy. Separated from the rest of his family, Grover shared a room above the store with another boy. Each slept in a rope bed covered with a straw mattress. The boys rose before six each morning, washed outside in the village horse trough, then swept and straightened the store before the seven o'clock opening hour. During the day they waited on customers, ran errands, made deliveries, and unloaded merchandise. Meals were taken whenever convenient, and it was a weary Grover Cleveland who climbed into bed each night at nine.

The routine quickly grew monotonous, and Grover

sensed that he must find something else to keep his mind active. While at Clinton Academy, he had enjoyed studying about ancient Greek and Roman philosophers and orators. On his own, Grover organized a debating group consisting of Fayetteville boys who came to the general store each week. They talked about current events in the country, argued their ideas, and discussed the government. Carefully Grover set aside his salary, eagerly planning to attend Hamilton College in Clinton the first chance he could.

A Death in the Family

The work at the American Home Missionary Society demanded long hours and extensive travel for Reverend Cleveland. Despite his belief in the agency, he could not maintain the tremendous pace required. So he accepted a call to the ministry of a church in Holland Patent, New York. Only weeks after assuming the pulpit in the small church, Reverend Cleveland suddenly collapsed while delivering a Sunday morning sermon. Within minutes he was dead.

Ann Cleveland was left a widow with four young children still at home. Sixteen-year-old Grover faced an important decision—whether to return home and help his mother or continue his plans to enroll at Hamilton College. Family responsibility won out, and the funds he had set aside for his education were added to the family's coffers.

Not wanting to return to Fayetteville, Grover accepted an offer to help one of his brothers work with the children at the New York Institution for the Blind in New York City. The work was grueling, with a schedule that would have challenged the most trained professional, much less a well-intentioned adolescent. "There is so much I wish I knew," Grover wrote home to his mother. "I am teaching reading, writing, numbers, history and geography. The boys and girls try so hard but no task is an easy one." Even in the sparkling sunlight, the institute's three-story, gray Gothic walls resembled a dismal tombstone.

Grover remained at the Institution for the Blind for a year, returning to Holland Patent in the fall of 1854. Members of the church had allowed his mother and the children to remain in the rectory at no charge. Grover quickly settled into helping his brothers and sisters with their schoolwork, and he began studying Latin with a local teacher. He also traveled to nearby Syracuse and Utica in hopes of finding full-time employment, but his lack of a college education prevented him from obtaining the positions he wanted. Letters sent to employers in the area met with similar negative results. "Go back to school," friends advised him. "You need that education."

ON TO BUFFALO

Many people were traveling west. Stories of new lands and jobs drifted through New York. Although Grover had hoped to stay close to home, there seemed no way to do it. He had an uncle living in Cleveland, Ohio, who was an engineer. Maybe his uncle could find a job for a willing-to-work boy of 18. After all, since that city had been settled by some distant relatives, there was a chance, Grover thought, that he could work and go to school there. A friend from Holland Patent agreed to travel west with Grover. They set out, each carrying $25 of borrowed money. Soon they hoped to double and triple their funds.

Thankfully, the countryside was dotted with Grover's relatives. Everywhere the two young men journeyed, they were greeted with happy smiles, hot meals, and warm beds. Nevertheless, their money still managed to trickle away. When they reached Buffalo, Grover and his friend hoped to find work riding barges on the Erie Canal so they could earn money to go to Cleveland. But first, Grover wanted to visit his Uncle Lewis in Buffalo.

Lewis F. Allen was well known to the people in the Buffalo area as a successful stockbreeder. His home in the Black Rock district along the Niagara River was considered a showplace. When Grover had visited his uncle five years before, every minute had been exciting. Yes, Uncle Lewis was definitely on the boy's list of people to see. He might even have some useful and new ideas. But when Uncle Lewis heard of Grover's plans to go to Cleveland, the older man was shocked. "Why do you want to head west? I can give you work right here in Buffalo."

Grover shook his head. "I don't know anything about breeding stock." Uncle Lewis leaned far back in his chair behind the desk. "I don't need you for that, boy. But you're good with words. Every year I've got to update my herdbook for other breeders. I'll pay you $50 a month for helping with the book, and you know you've got free room and board. How does that sound?"

It was not a difficult decision for Grover to make. After all, there was no sure job waiting for him in Ohio. The food on his uncle's table was plentiful and tasty, the bed had a mattress of genuine goose feathers, and $50 would give him enough money to send some of it home. The boy nodded. "I accept your offer," Grover said, "and I'm grateful for it."

Grover took to the new task eagerly. He enjoyed learning and working with words. Visiting the 600-acre farm where his uncle raised shorthorn and Devon cattle offered a cheerful break from his work. Life was seldom dull.

Buffalo was a rapidly growing city in 1855. With over 55,000 residents, it also claimed distinction as a transportation hub of the country. Goods were shipped west from the city across the Great Lakes, while railroads fed into the city from the east and south. The Erie Canal offered a direct waterway to New York City.

Learning the Law

After giving much thought about his future, Grover concluded that the study of law would be an attractive career. That decision was based on his past experiences. Some of his favorite moments had been with the debating group in Fayetteville. And while at Clinton Academy, he had enjoyed studying about the laws and orators of the ancient Greek and Roman civilizations. Moreover, a college education was not required in order to become a lawyer. In fact, many apprentices studied law by working actively with established, practicing attorneys.

When Grover sought his uncle's advice, the older man could not hide his disappointment. "I'd hoped you might take to raising stock," Uncle Lewis responded. But he honored his nephew's choice and agreed to set up appointments with attorneys around Buffalo.

Grover's first interview did not go very well. Justice Daniel Hibbard asked a lot of personal questions. Annoyed with the interrogation, Grover stormed out of the office. "A good attorney must be able to control his temper," his uncle counseled. "But you do have a right to privacy, as does any citizen."

Grover next went to visit Henry W. Rogers, head of the distinguished law firm of Rogers, Bowen and Rogers. It was immediately evident that the gruff Rogers had little interest in training law clerks but was only interviewing Cleveland as a courtesy to Uncle Lewis. Nevertheless, Grover was told to report the next day to begin his apprenticeship.

When the eager and enthusiastic young Cleveland arrived at the office the next day, he was met by a scowling Rogers. Handing Grover a thick, black volume, the attorney ordered, "Read this from cover to cover." Leading the way to a small, dusty table in the back of the office, Rogers added, "And try to stay out of the way of the people working around here."

Grover took the thick, heavy book and sat down at the table. "Will I be able to work with any of the lawyers? Do I just have to sit here reading? I had hoped when you said I could be . . ." The glowering look on Henry Rogers' face made Grover stop in mid-sentence. He gazed down at Grover. "The book you're holding is Blackstone's *Commentaries*," said Rogers, each word carefully measured. "It is the cornerstone of English law, the foundation of all law as we practice it. Before you begin pestering our attorneys with foolish questions, read this book. Do you understand?"

Grover gulped deeply. "Y-Yes, sir."

It was not the start Grover had hoped for. Yet he knew his place from the very beginning. He soon learned that Rogers, Bowen and Rogers was one of the most respected law firms in the country. Millard Fillmore, who had served as President of the United States from 1850 to 1853, had been a member of this firm.

Each day Grover waded through more pages of Blackstone's *Commentaries*. He was fascinated with the cases and decisions. Sometimes he imagined himself speaking for a client. Everyone strained to hear his words. Even the judge leaned forward, captivated by the wisdom of the great attorney, Grover Cleveland.

Other clerks came into the law offices of Rogers, Bowen and Rogers, but no one worked as hard as Grover. He requested permission to attend some of the firm's cases when they went to court. He compared what he saw and heard with cases in Blackstone's *Commentaries*. Grover also volunteered to run errands for the firm's attorneys. Soon he was looking up past cases for background and helping prepare simple legal papers.

There was no clock-watching for Grover Cleveland, no effort to slip out of any extra work. He spent many nights working at the office. He even took a room in town so he would waste less time getting to and from work. However, his uncle did not think that this was a good idea. "That's not a wise decision," Lewis Allen declared. "Buffalo is not safe at night."

Grover nodded, knowing what his uncle said was true. Hardly a night went by when someone wasn't murdered, often in one of the saloons near the law offices. Still, Grover stood firm. "I can take care of myself," he answered. It was difficult to argue with him. At this time he was well over six feet tall and weighed 220 pounds.

Transitions, Personal and Political

The year 1856 brought a major change in American politics. A new party organization, the Republicans, replaced the group formerly known as the Whigs. Lewis Allen, Henry Rogers, and almost everyone else Grover knew in Buffalo had been Whigs. Now they became Republicans. Dennis Bowen, a partner in the law firm, switched from Whig to Democrat. Grover followed Bowen's political lead. He liked James Buchanan, the Democratic candidate for President, and was delighted when Buchanan won.

Knowing that some of his decisions had strained relationships with his uncle, Grover attempted to repair the damage. He began spending more time at the Allen farm at Black Rock. He helped the farmhands with the crops and gave the herdbook his dedicated attention.

Although he spent most of his free time working at the farm, Grover also found time for fishing in the lakes and ponds that dotted the farm. All the farmhands knew that if the fish were biting, Grover Cleveland could always find the best spots.

As the days slipped by, however, Grover spent less and less time on the farm. The tests for admission to the New York bar were coming up, and he had to prepare for them. Grover wanted to be ready so he could tell his family in Holland Patent that he had passed the bar. His mother was proud of Grover. Each month he sent home a sizable part of his salary. She knew he was spending his days working as hard as possible, studying and helping in the law office.

Whether Grover's mother would have been equally proud of his nightlife is more doubtful. As he entered his 20s, Grover became a more frequent customer of the saloons and dancehalls in Buffalo. Chubbiness turned to fat as Grover drank huge quantities of beer. An ever-growing stomach hung over pants straining to hold their seams. Grover grew a moustache, at first neat and trimmed, but gradually becoming more like walrus whiskers. Surrounded by companions, he drank and sang many nights away. And when his friends staggered home for sleep, Grover simply replaced beer with coffee. After splashing cold water on his face and tossing down five cups of coffee, Grover was ready to face another day at the office.

"I don't see how the fellow does it," another law clerk observed. "He doesn't seem to need any sleep at all."

A Lawyer at Last

In 1859 Grover Cleveland was officially accepted into the New York Bar Association. Attorneys in the firm of Rogers, Bowen and Rogers praised their young law clerk highly. He was earning $600 a year.

One night Grover stood at the window of the law office. Now 22 years old, he knew it was time to make another big decision. He felt comfortable in Buffalo and had no desire to leave. Yet he felt an urge to try something new, to test his talents further. A heavy fog enveloped the building in which Grover stood. He shook his head. His future was just as murky as the air outside.

Chapter 3
Word Wizard

"**H**ave you ever thought about politics?" The question came from Dennis Bowen. The middle partner of Rogers, Bowen and Rogers leaned over Grover's desk, waiting for a reply. Sitting back in his chair, Grover pondered his answer.

Politics. He liked working with people, listening to their thoughts and needs. He had done a bit of low-level work with the Democratic Party in Buffalo, reminding voters in the second ward to go to the polls on election day. He did like any task that involved meeting new people. "Well, there's a lot I like about politics," Grover answered. "Were you thinking about me doing more work for the party or becoming a candidate for office sometime?"

Bowen smiled. "Yes and yes. I mean, why not both? Let me be honest with you, Grover. A lot of fellows come to clerk in a law firm. Some want to show off in a courtroom. Others want to get rich. Most want to run for some kind of political office. You're different. You're efficient and able, willing to give your best to the most tiresome assignment. You're a wizard with words too."

Grover nodded his thanks. He knew he was not brilliant. Certainly he did not have the education he would have liked. Yet he did find handling a last will and testament just as exciting as working with a client accused of murder. Both were vital tasks within the law. He did not mind long hours, tedious details.

Grover sat forward. "All right, let's say I'm interested. Where do we go from here?"

Dennis Bowen stood up. A wide smile crossed his face as he extended his hand to Grover. "That's all I need to know for now. It's just, as 10th ward alderman, I may be able to put in a few good words for you. I had to know what you thought about it first. Not everyone's cut out for politics, but I think you are." "I appreciate your interest," said Grover. "Keep me posted on any news."

Grover Cleveland kept building his reputation at Rogers, Bowen and Rogers. His annual salary climbed to over $1,000. It was money gratefully received by his mother in Holland Patent, and carefully dispensed among the Cleveland family.

SHADOWS OF WAR

Beyond the boundaries of Buffalo and Holland Patent, turmoil was brewing in the United States. During ordinary times, James Buchanan might have been a most effective President. He was known as a master of compromise, always able to bring disagreeing factions together. The issues, however, seemed now to have gone beyond compromise. Political leaders argued heatedly in Washington. Some stood solidly behind slavery; others stood just as solidly against it. There was just as much disagreement over what constitutional powers the national government had and which ones were reserved to the individual states.

When President Buchanan announced that he would not seek a second term, the Democrats were stunned. The news saddened Grover, who felt that Buchanan might be able to dispel the war clouds that were forming. Instead, Republican Abraham Lincoln was elected. "At least he believes in a strong union of states," Grover told his friends. "The federal government will remain strong. Lincoln will see to it." But it would not happen without a struggle. On the heels of Lincoln's inauguration, the Civil War broke out.

Across the country men signed up to fight when President Lincoln issued a call for volunteers. Grover weighed the decision. There were a number of points to consider, many of them concerned with his family. "Your brothers Lewis and Richard have enlisted to fight for the North," wrote his mother from Holland Patent. "I think young Fred may also. I pray you will not be so moved. There is surely a better way to solve problems than by killing. We do so depend upon your support."

Grover did not take his family obligations lightly. There were also political doors that were swinging open to him. In 1862, Dennis Bowen sponsored Grover as a delegate to the Democratic city convention in Buffalo. The good job he had done in ward politics helped him win a spot as a supervisor.

Political leaders in Erie County were hearing more and more about the industrious lawyer at Rogers, Bowen and Rogers. When the position of assistant district attorney opened up, Grover was asked to take the job. He was glad to accept, putting aside all thoughts of joining in the war effort. There would continue to be money to send home, too.

The job of assistant district attorney was more work than Grover had expected. Because his supervisor, District Attorney Torrance, was old and sickly, most of the legal duties fell to Grover. Always there was another case to write up, another document to file. Some nights Grover got no sleep at all.

To Fight or Not to Fight

As the Civil War continued, a draft call went out throughout the northern states. In every community, names of all men fit for military service were put inside a drum-shaped box.

Then the names were drawn out as the box turned slowly on an axle. If a man's name was drawn and he chose not to serve, he could pay a substitute to serve for him. Grover's name was among the first pulled from the draft box. The district attorney did not want Grover to go. "Anybody can carry a gun. Few men can do the work you do," Torrance told Grover. "Plan to hire a substitute. There are plenty of men who would go. His younger brother Fred immediately offered to go in his place. "Mother counts on your help," Fred declared. "I'm not working. I'll go."

It was a generous offer. Yet Grover would not accept it. Fred had already served some time in the army.

Once again Grover pondered the situation. To fight or not to fight—that was the question. No one believed more strongly than he in a strong union of states tied together by the federal government. To cut the country up, as southern leaders suggested, was like hacking pieces out of a perfect pie. The Union was a cause worth defending, Cleveland thought.

But Grover knew that his mother and the three Cleveland children still at home depended on the money he sent them. There was also much truth in what District Attorney Torrance said. Many men could carry guns, but Grover was doing specialized legal work that only he could do. After careful thought, Grover visited the draft service office. In his pocket he had the $300 to buy a substitute. It was borrowed money, but he could earn it back.

Toward an Election

More than ever, Grover threw himself into the work at the district attorney's office. Another assistant, Lyman Bass, became a good friend and roommate.

In 1865, the Civil War dragged to a weary end. Unfortunately, President Lincoln had no opportunity to lead in the rebuilding of the nation. He was shot down by an assassin on April 14 and died early the next morning. In Buffalo, meanwhile, Grover Cleveland took another step in his move up the political ladder. He agreed to be the candidate for district attorney on the Democratic ticket. His opponent? None other than his roommate and friend, Lyman K. Bass.

It was a low-key election, without the excitement of open public debates. Most of the speeches were given in Buffalo saloons, with the sounds of dancehall music and clanging beer mugs in the background. Grover knew it was an uphill battle because Buffalo boasted a heavy Republican population. When the votes were counted, Grover's worries were confirmed. He had won the city vote, but outlying farmers followed the Republican ticket. Graciously, Grover congratulated his roommate and cleaned out his own desk at the district attorney's office.

On His Own

For the first time since he had started to study law, Grover was now completely on his own. There was no one to look over his shoulder or assign him duties. He was his own boss. It gave him a new desire to succeed, to distinguish himself within his profession. Grover like the feeling and set up his own private practice.

However, he had no intention of dropping out of politics. Running for district attorney had been just a beginning. The young lawyer knew there would be other chances in the future. Shrewdly, Grover charted his course within the framework of the Democratic Party. He stayed in touch with other Democrats while maintaining a busy law practice. His good reputation attracted the attention of other Buffalo attorneys. Two of them, Albert Lanin and Oscar Folsom, were known for their honesty and many influential business contacts. When they came to Grover and suggested merging their legal talents, he accepted.

Grover had little interest in spectacular criminal cases.

He preferred quiet cases, working behind the scenes on civil matters. "You can't lose when Cleveland's working for you," residents of Buffalo would say. "He's honest and has just the right way with words."

One man came to Grover complaining about a dead horse. "I just bought the mare a week ago and now she's dead. Can I get my money back?" Grover took the case, only to find the judge ruling against him. "There was no promise the horse would live for a day or a year," the judge declared. The verdict disappointed Grover, yet he went out that night and won another horse for his client in a card game. He wanted no one saying he had lost the case.

Another case involved a woman who was ordered from her home because she fell behind in her mortgage payments. Although she had three children, the law was against her. Fortunately for her, Grover Cleveland was not. He promptly paid off her mortgage.

"His heart's in the right place," Buffalo people said. "Got a good head for big business, too."

There was no doubt about that. With Lanin and Folsom bringing in major railway contacts, Grover became skilled at handling million-dollar accounts. Quickly Buffalo expanded its position as a transportation hub of the country, thanks in part to Cleveland's shrewd legal talent. When members of the Democratic Party asked Grover to take over leadership of the party in Erie County, Grover politely refused. The job would take too much time from his work.

He did, however, take time to attend the state Democratic convention in 1868. Although he said little, preferring just to observe, there were people at the convention who were observing him. The name of Grover Cleveland was acquiring a reputation around the state, a reputation based on integrity and fair legal practices.

CLIMBING THE POLITICAL LADDER

Two years later, in 1870, Grover was visited by two leaders of the state Democratic Party. They wasted no words as they sat in his law office. "We've come here to get you to run for United States Congress," one of the visitors declared. "You have a reputation for honesty and hard work. As our candidate, we would give you all the help we can." Grover rested the fingers of his right hand against the right side of his bushy moustache. "I'll confess I have an itch to run for office again. But I was thinking of throwing my hat into the sheriff's race around here."

The visitors exchanged surprised looks. The sheriff's race seldom attracted professional men, especially lawyers. It was a job for a political hack. Certainly the salary was attractive enough. Still, it meant rubbing elbows with many of Buffalo's undesirables, such as the thieves and drunks who roamed the waterfront district.

"We'd like to make some reforms in national government," the second visitor continued. "We need someone who . . ."

Grover shook his head. "I'm sorry, gentlemen. I've made up my mind. Maybe another time . . ."

The Sheriff of Erie County

At the age of 33, Grover Cleveland became a candidate for sheriff of Erie County. Because he had friends in both political parties, it was hardly a contest. After winning by a margin of several hundred votes, he threw a boisterous victory party.

Grover carefully looked over the duties of the sheriff's office. He realized it was very important that he find a good undersheriff. Once that was done, Grover did what he had never done before — he relaxed.

Sheriffs who had held the job before him encouraged

In 1871, the year Grover Cleveland was elected sheriff of Erie County, New York, cartoonist Thomas Nast created the lasting symbol for Cleveland's political party—the Democratic donkey. (Library of Congress.)

Grover to do just that. "The office runs itself," one of his predecessors told him. "If you have other things you'd rather do, go ahead and enjoy yourself. Do it." It was welcome advice to a man who had seldom wasted a minute of his life. Grover set responsibility aside. He headed for the best fishing spots in the area. When he wasn't reeling in a catch for the day, he was playing cards with his friends.

"Is There No Honesty Left"

However, sometimes Grover had to deal with uncomfortable situations. Democratic Party leaders kept sending him men to hire. Often the men were not suited or trained for the jobs they were supposed to fill. Civil service—the selecting of workers based on merit and ability—was only in its early stages. Patronage—giving jobs to family, friends, and members of the same political party—was the dominant practice.

Grover bucked the patronage system. He refused to accept men for jobs just because they had the Democratic Party's stamp of approval. "I can tell if a person can handle the work," he told party officials. "Let me do the job I was elected to do."

Grover's attitude lost him influential supporters in the party. He annoyed others when he started checking up on Democrats who had contracts with the county. Food merchants were not delivering to the jails what their contracts required. Supplies of firewood ran short for the same reason. "Is there no honesty left around here?" he demanded to know. "Just look the other way," he was told.

Unpleasant Tasks

Grover refused. Not only did he push the practice of hiring based only on ability, he also broke contracts with those who cheated the county. He opened trades and services to public bidding, then accepted the best offers. Criticism, even threats, came from other county officials. "I've got a job to do," Sheriff Cleveland declared. "It might be easier to do it differently, but I'll take the bad chores with the good."

One of the most unpleasant duties of the sheriff's office was to carry out executions. Because it was not a job most sheriffs wanted to do, the task usually fell to an undersheriff or deputy. Grover, however, took the role of executioner on

In 1874, while Cleveland was practicing law in Buffalo, New York, cartoonist Thomas Nast provided the Republican Party with their symbol—a thundering elephant. (Library of Congress.)

himself. "The people elected me, and I'll do what needs to be done." While Grover Cleveland was sheriff of Erie County, he was called on twice to execute men. He carried out his promise, but each time he became sick afterwards.

As he ended his two-year term in office, Grover had no desire to run again. The bickering with and criticism from his Democratic peers soured him on the job. They were equally pleased with his decision because he stood too firm on his principles of honesty. He was not willing to take orders often enough.

Leaving the sheriff's post, Grover was discouraged and disgruntled. Still, it had not been a totally bad experience. The money he sent home had enabled his mother and family to enjoy security. In addition, Grover had saved $20,000 for himself.

Back to Private Practice

When his friend and former roommate, Lyman Bass, approached him about setting up a law practice together, Grover eagerly accepted. Both men had found the political system not to their liking. They also shared common beliefs, one being that the law should not be abused by people in power. Most people knew that Grover Cleveland was a Democrat and Lyman Bass was a Republican. However, both men were considered hardworking and honest. That reputation brought a steady stream of clients into their office.

Despite a busy law practice, Grover frequently visited Buffalo restaurants and saloons. As his weight continued to mushroom, his size earned him the nicknames "Big Grove" and "Big Cleve."

It was a mixed collection of people who went in and out of the 700 saloons in Buffalo. Naturally, more prominent members of society frequented the quieter drinking places, removed from the crudities of the lower class. Grover, however, played no favorites. He enjoyed the company of businessmen, many of whom were his clients, and he helped organize the City Club of Buffalo, a private club catering to the wealthy and elite of the area. Yet he felt equally at home among the rowdier elements of Buffalo society.

There were also women who looked upon the successful lawyer as possible husband material. Although Grover may not have been the most physically attractive man in Buffalo, he was always well dressed and properly mannered. Some said he even went fishing in his usual attire of black suit, white linen shirt, and necktie.

One woman who was attracted to Grover was Maria Crofts Halpin, a popular young widow from Pennsylvania who enjoyed the company of many men. When they met in 1873, the smiling Grover Cleveland could not know then just how great an impact Maria would have on his life.

Chapter 4

Chasing the Foxes

During the daytime, Maria Crofts Halpin worked in a Buffalo department store. It was no easy task raising two young children on her wages. Each evening she left her children with friends and enjoyed the city's nightlife. She looked more like 25 than 35. Her laugh came quickly, her eyes sparkled, and she never sat alone for long.

Grover Cleveland was just one of the many men who found Maria good company. After long days of scanning legal reports and talking to clients, he was happy to find someone who knew nothing about the law. Maria lived in an apartment not far from his, and Grover frequently took the widow home.

UNEXPECTED FATHERHOOD

In the spring of 1874, Maria announced that she was pregnant. The news stunned Grover. She claimed he was the father. It was a possibility, of course, he knew that. It was also just as possible the father could be someone else. Grover Cleveland was not the only gentleman friend of Maria Crofts Halpin. Still, he was the only bachelor who was seeing her. All her other male friends were married and had families.

"Well, what do you propose to do?" Maria asked Cleveland.

"I'll need to think about it," he answered.

There was no question of marriage. Although she was a lively companion, Maria Crofts Halpin was not the kind of woman Grover Cleveland wanted for a wife. So, instead of marrying Maria, he assumed financial responsibility for both mother and child.

In the years that followed, Cleveland kept a close watch on Maria and her son. It became clear that she was ill-suited to be a mother. When news reached him of how she was mistreating her children, Cleveland took legal action. After she was committed to an institution where she could get help, her children were adopted by parents deemed fit to raise them. The boy who was supposedly Cleveland's son eventually became a physician.

Cleveland suffered another shocking blow in the 1870s. His brothers, Cecil and Fred, lost their lives aboard the steamship *Missouri* when it burned and sank in the Bahama Islands. Both men had been contributing financially to their mother. With them gone, the entire responsibility fell on Grover.

Tragedy struck again when Cleveland's former law partner and good friend, Oscar Folsom, was killed in a buggy accident. Grover managed the family's legal matters and became guardian to Folsom's 10-year-old daughter, Frances. "I have as many family responsibilities as most men," Cleveland told people who asked why he did not marry. "Anyway, I think I'll just wait until little Frances grows up and then marry her." Everyone laughed at the remark. Everyone, that is, except Grover Cleveland.

The law firm of Bass and Cleveland continued to attract new business. Another partner, Wilson Bissell, was added, and trainees came to study, just as Cleveland had done 20 years before. In 1877, Bass was forced to seek a better climate due to tuberculosis, so he moved to Colorado Springs. By 1880, it was clear that another partner was needed, so the firm became Cleveland, Bissell and Sicard.

THE RELUCTANT MAYOR

As Cleveland's reputation as a lawyer beamed brighter, politics in Buffalo dimmed even more. No matter which political party controlled city offices, citizens paid more taxes and received fewer services. People on street corners spoke openly of the corruption strangling local government. Every now and then someone would say, "Why doesn't the federal government step in and do something?"

Sadly, what was happening in Buffalo was also happening in Washington, but on an even greater scale. The two terms of the Grant administration, from March 1869 until March 1877, were filled with officials willing to sell and trade public lands to make their own private fortunes. Illegal schemes were handled more smoothly at the national level; they were just more widely known and talked about at the city level.

Political corruption was accepted as part of daily life in Buffalo. Certainly Cleveland was not blind to what was happening in the city government, but he still had a bad taste in his mouth from his experience as sheriff. He also had friends in the city and county political parties but participated very little in regular Democratic activities.

A ray of hope appeared in 1881 when Peter Doyle was picked to lead the Democratic Party in Erie County. A good friend of Cleveland's, Doyle was known for his honesty and ability to get things done.

"The first thing we need to find in Buffalo is a good candidate for mayor," Doyle declared. "Then we need to kick all the crooked rats out!" Immediately the crusader formed a committee to get started, but the task was easier said than done. Doyle and his supporters combed the city, hoping to find an honest businessman who would run. Each time the answer was "No." Corruption had been associated with the position too long. Individuals with excellent reputations had no interest in risking their good name. Some were willing to put up money for someone else to run, but finding a good candidate seemed impossible.

For days Doyle and his friends tried every method of persuasion they knew. Each night, after 10 straight hours of visiting potential candidates, they would sit around a restaurant table and pore over lists of names, wearily scratching out those they had already contacted.

A Formidable Candidate

It was on just such an evening that Grover Cleveland walked into the restaurant where Doyle and his friends were meeting. Doyle's eyes widened as he nodded toward his lawyer friend. The others at the table exchanged looks. At once, each had the same thought: Grover Cleveland for mayor! There was no rule that the candidate *had* to be a businessman.

It was said that Cleveland ran one of the best law offices in the state. He was known within the Democratic Party. Though not everyone liked him, those who didn't were the ones he had caught cheating the county when he was sheriff. One thing was certain—with over 250 pounds resting on a six-foot frame, Grover Cleveland would indeed be a formidable candidate! Motioning him to their table, Doyle wasted no time in asking. Cleveland wasted no time in answering. "I'm not interested," he said firmly. "Find somebody else."

In the hours that followed, Doyle and his friends appealed to Cleveland's sense of public service, his ego, his willingness to accept a challenge. Slowly, ever so slowly, his resistance faded. The law practice would be there, win or lose. Anyway, he thought, it would be worth a try to get rid of some of the no-good loafers in city government who did nothing but line their pockets with the people's money.

It was almost daybreak when Cleveland made his decision. He would run—but on one condition. He wanted the right to approve everyone else who would be running on the ticket with him. After all, if there was going to be good government in Buffalo, lots of changes would have to be made. It was time for reform, so new faces and honest programs were needed. Doyle agreed to Cleveland's condition, pledging support of the Democratic Party.

Cleveland entered the campaign like a bull charging into a bullfight. He drew up a framework for city government based on sound business practices. Records were to be kept of every transaction. Money could not be spent that the city did not have. Workers would be paid once a week rather than once a month. Regular inspections would be made to see that all city offices were carrying out their duties.

The campaign became vicious. "Swindlers!" shouted the Republicans at the Democrats. "Thieves!" the Democrats yelled back. One accusation followed another. Political debates ended up in wild brawls, but Cleveland never backed away from a fight. He would often stand on tabletops in restaurants and saloons and hurl angry challenges at Republicans. But he played no favorites. He also shouted out the names of fellow Democrats who had violated their responsibilities in office.

In November of 1881, the voters went to the polls. Republicans swept the state office positions, but Cleveland captured the mayor's chair by 3,600 votes. He pulled other Democrats in with him at the city level. Clearly, the people of Buffalo wanted some changes, and Grover Cleveland was ready to provide the reforms. From the moment he was sworn in on January 1, 1882, he made no secret he was prepared to start cleaning house—or rather, city hall.

"You have elected me to protect your tax money and to make sure your lives are served by officials deserving of your trust," Cleveland told the people. "It will mean chasing the foxes out of the henhouse. You know who they are and I know who they are. They might want to start running now because I'll be coming to get them with a shotgun." The people chuckled at their new mayor's words. But they were soon to learn he meant what he said, much to the discomfort of the political "foxes."

On the Attack

Cleveland got right to work. One of his first targets was the Buffalo Street Department. Private contractors overcharged the city 10 cents a foot for every sidewalk laid on city property. No one inspected the work after it was completed, nor did anyone check the bills submitted. "We'll be doing that a little differently from now on," Cleveland told department officials. "You'd better be certain all your numbers are correct."

Sewage was another problem. Over 1,300 residents of Buffalo died of epidemic diseases in 1880. Typhoid fever, often carried in sewage, was the biggest killer. There seemed to be no effective solution. The core of the problem was finding the proper place for the city's sewage. Both Lake Erie and the Erie Canal had been tried, but there were obstacles to using either waterway. Because Cleveland felt it was too big a problem for Buffalo to handle by itself, he decided to call on the state of New York for help.

The city engineer and members of the city council were outraged. "We can take care of our own business!" the councilmen stormed. They threatened to block all the mayor's future plans. Supported by the Buffalo newspapers, Cleveland stuck to his guns. When a state senator took the mayor's sewage program and his plan for a sewage commission to the capital in Albany, the state legislature created the commission Cleveland requested.

Disgruntled councilmen attempted to stall Cleveland's proposals. They insisted on a long-term bond program to finance the new sewage system. "It's great for private investors," declared the mayor, "but it's lousy for the people of Buffalo." He vetoed the council's action, demanding a quicker, more simple financing program. To show their displeasure, the councilmen rejected the names Cleveland submitted to be members of the sewage commission. Not discouraged, the mayor returned the list to the council for their approval.

Learning more and more about politics, Cleveland realized he could not win his battles without the support of the citizens of Buffalo. To reach the people, he had to have the newspapers on his side. Cleveland met with editors and reporters, giving them interviews and explaining his plans for progress and reform in Buffalo. Political cartoonists depicted the lone Cleveland fighting the 26 men on the city council. Big as he was, Cleveland still appeared as one man against a mob.

With the people of Buffalo behind him, Cleveland intensified his efforts to improve the city. He vetoed bill after bill that favored individuals over the public welfare. No longer could councilmen slip through their own pet projects. "If it doesn't make Buffalo a better city, forget it!" Cleveland blustered. "Some of these bills you send me stink like skunks in the woodpile."

Although Cleveland usually had the people on his side, now and then he took on the residents of Buffalo, too. When he proposed a city water system to replace free water wells, many citizens protested. They did not have to pay for well water but fees were charged for city water. "Too many wells are contaminated," argued Cleveland. "If you won't protect yourselves, someone will have to." The mayor won.

"A Public Office . . . A Public Trust"

George Talbot little suspected what he was taking on when he submitted a bid of $422,500 to keep Buffalo's streets clean for five years. Although another bidder promised to do the same job for $313,500, Talbot's bid was accepted by the city council. It was not accepted by the mayor, however. Cleveland challenged the bid publicly, demanding to know all the details. Some councilmen tried to protect themselves, but Cleveland would not be put off. "A public office is a public trust," he told reporters. "Anyone betraying that trust is a common criminal."

Cleveland's words echoed across the nation, bringing nods of agreement everywhere, including Washington. After vetoing the council's acceptance of Talbot's bid, Cleveland led the fight to offer the street cleaning job to the lowest bidder. Clearly, the mayor had given the people of Buffalo what they wanted—a leader willing to make sweeping changes and clean up the city.

There were people outside of Buffalo, who noticed the rotund but dynamic Democratic champion, Grover Cleveland. "A public office is a public trust." Those words had a nice ring to them. Why, it could even become a catchy slogan for someone running for higher office. Maybe the governorship of New York. And then, who knows where the path might lead . . .

Chapter 5

"Big Enough for Any Job"

Grover Cleveland liked being the mayor of Buffalo. He even enjoyed the skirmishes, those fiery encounters and exchanges with members of the city council. But it was not his usual style or choice to give speeches. Rather, he preferred things on paper, whether they were proposals he wanted the council to accept or proposals from the council he chose to veto.

But the quality of Buffalo's city council members — or perhaps the lack of quality — offered Cleveland a chance to appear more dazzling than he might otherwise have seemed. Always prepared, he was able to look at all aspects of matters being discussed. Often the councilmen were clearly uninformed and bungling. They had not done "their homework," and it showed. Questions were left unanswered, problems unsolved. Cleveland refused to sign any city rules or laws that were unclear or incomplete.

IN A POSITION TO RISE

When he became the mayor of Buffalo, Grover Cleveland had no future plans to climb the political ladder to higher positions. Most often, state representatives and senators in Congress move up to governor or even President. A mayor's office is usually a dead end politically. By 1881, only one President out of 20 had been a mayor. That was Andrew Johnson, who had served as the mayor of Greeneville, Tennessee.

In Cleveland's time, a city mayor's post seldom attracted top leaders. The salary for the job was notoriously low. Cleveland, for example, earned $2,500 a year, but he probably would have served as mayor for free. Fortunately, he could maintain an active interest in his law firm. This allowed him to build a small fortune for the times.

Politics affect people in different ways. Some think there are too many negatives to holding public office: friends seeking favors, public arguments, newspaper criticism. All these pressures, and more, cause many would-be politicians to withdraw from the limelight. But not Cleveland. He could say no as easily to a friend as to an enemy. He enjoyed open and free discussion about an issue. And he welcomed newspaper comments, insisting that he had a right to challenge the press about accurate coverage of opinions and events.

As the mayor of Buffalo, Grover Cleveland did not emerge as a crusader. Instead, he brought a conscience to politics. It may have been the strict moral codes of childhood that he learned in a minister's household. Or maybe it was instinct, a peculiar sense with which Cleveland was born.

The conscience that guided Cleveland as mayor made him very sensitive to the public. He evaluated everything the city did on the basis of its effect on the city's citizens – the poor and powerless as well as the rich and powerful. He saw himself as a protector, making certain no one, or at least as few as possible, suffered.

Turbulent Times

During ordinary times, it is unlikely Grover Cleveland would have been thrust so suddenly into the political spotlight. But the times were not ordinary. On July 2, 1881, President James

Garfield was shot down by an assassin in Washington, D.C. He lingered near death until September 19, when he passed away in his sleep. A Republican, Garfield was succeeded by Chester A. Arthur, considered by many to be a weak leader and easily beatable by a Democrat in the presidential contest of 1884.

As the state with the largest population, New York often furnished candidates for presidential contests. The governor's position was considered by many to be a springboard into the race for the nation's chief executive's job. So, early in 1882, as the Democrats in New York discussed potential candidates for governor of their state, they knew their decision might affect the nation's future. The times demanded a wise choice for governor. But whom?

Roswell Flower had a strong following. A young, rich, and popular financier from New York City, he had served the party well. Another strong contender was General Henry Slocum of Brooklyn. A Civil War leader, he appealed to those voters stirred by patriotism. "Why, Slocum marched with General Sherman through Georgia in the war," a supporter would declare. It was enough to win applause and attention.

Democratic leaders of Tammany Hall, the organization that controlled New York City politics, were not happy with either Flower or Slocum. Neither seemed to be a sure winner, and that's all the Tammany Hall people wanted so they could control the governorship.

Grover Cleveland's mind was not on state politics in the early spring and summer of 1882. Much of his time was spent in Holland Patent, where Ann Cleveland was dying. His mother had always encouraged Grover to reach for high goals. When she died on July 19, 1882, Cleveland pledged to continue reaching.

For 10 years Edgar Apgar, a Democratic Party worker, had been following Cleveland's career. Even when Cleveland was sheriff of Erie County, the politically astute Apgar was pushing Cleveland to climb the political ladder. But Cleveland refused to be pushed.

"If someone wants me to do something, he can come to me and ask," Cleveland declared. "Being mayor of Buffalo is all that a man could ask for. I am content."

The words sounded almost convincing. Yet, there was little doubt that Cleveland was carefully watching the political developments within the state Democratic Party. Shortly before the New York State Democratic Convention in September 1882, Cleveland made his move. He called in his friends and supporters. "I'm willing to run for governor if the delegates want me, " he told them.

REACHING FOR THE STATEHOUSE

Both the Democratic and Republican state conventions met the same week in September 1882. The Republicans, meeting earlier in the week, quickly selected Charles Folger as their candidate. He was the clear choice of the business interests running the party machinery.

The Democrats, on the other hand, wanted to avoid picking a candidate who appeared to represent major political bosses, such as Tammany Hall. "We've got to select a candidate free from association with the wheeler-dealers within the party," noted one convention leader. "That way, we'll pick up some Republican votes from people tired of their own party machinery."

When the Democratic delegates assembled in Syracuse for their state convention, neither Flower nor Slocum had enough votes to capture the nomination. Not only that, both men had strong opponents who spoke against them. Insults flew back and forth; tempers flared. Edgar Apgar then called on the delegates, talking in favor of Cleveland. "He doesn't owe anything to anyone," Apgar insisted, sharing his vast knowledge of Cleveland's background. "The man is worshipped in Buffalo for cleaning up the whole city," Apgar said of Cleveland.

Some might have said that Apgar's claims were exaggerated, but they had the effect he hoped for. The delegates agreed to meet Cleveland, who was waiting to be invited to the convention. When the invitation came, he wasted no time boarding a train and heading to Syracuse, where a reception was hurriedly set up in a hotel lobby.

"Hello, I'm Grover Cleveland. Thank you for stopping by." Again and again Buffalo's mayor greeted delegates as they came by the hotel. His handshake was firm, his manner friendly and sincere. His portly frame was carefully tucked inside his finest black suit and white linen shirt. A simple gold tie tack accented a dark silk tie. There was no question that Grover Cleveland was trying to make a good impression. By the time he headed back to Buffalo early the next morning, he had met most of the 385 delegates attending the convention.

Nomination speeches were made. No one spoke more eloquently than Edgar Apgar. "Roswell Flower is a good man and Henry Slocum is a good man," Apgar noted. "Yet to nominate either one of these men would be to divide our noble political party. We need a candidate who will pull our party together. Then he will pull our state together. That man is Grover Cleveland!" Applause and cheering thundered in the convention center. Cleveland won on the third ballot.

At that time, nominated candidates did not attend their party's convention. Nor did they give public speeches during the campaign. The political parties took care of that. Across the state traveled supporters of Republican Charles

Folger and Democrat Grover Cleveland. It was a spirited campaign. "Folger's a puppet of big business!" stormed Democratic leaders. "If you elect him, you are picking Jay Gould, the railroad king, to run our state. Let's derail both of them!"

Republicans charged that "Cleveland's a nobody. The job is too big for him!" Such charges backfired. "Why, just look at Cleveland!" one man in an audience yelled back. "He's big enough for any job!" That remark spread quickly. "He's big enough for any job!" It was a natural as a catchy political slogan.

The voters cast their ballots in November. Cleveland solidly trounced Folger, rolling up a victory margin of 192,000 votes out of the 915,000 cast. Even Samuel Tilden, a notable Democratic chieftain, had only a 50,000-vote margin when he won the governorship a few years before. And since most governors outside the Democratic southern states were Republicans, Cleveland was clearly a force to be reckoned with in the future.

Bigger Job, Bigger Future

"Grover Cleveland of New York has not only won the governorship," wrote one newspaper editor, "he has won top billing as a future presidential candidate. Surely the Democrats are looking at him to carry the party banner in 1884."

Cleveland chuckled as he read such items. "Here are people speculating if I'll run for President when I haven't even been sworn in as governor yet. Politics is a funny business." Funny or not, Cleveland enjoyed the speculation. Certainly the thought of running for President was not offensive to him.

First, however, there was much to do in Albany, the state capital of New York. Cleveland hoped he had the ability required to live up to the voters' expectations. "I am honest and sincere in my desire to do well," he wrote his brother, William, "but the question is whether I know enough to accomplish what I desire."

There was only one way to find out. From the moment Cleveland was sworn in as governor on January 1, 1883, he tackled the responsibilities of the office with all the talent and time he had. Each day found Cleveland at his desk early after walking to his office from his living quarters in the governor's mansion. There were always stacks of papers to review, visitors to meet, and letters to write. He returned home to take his meals, but evenings often found him working past midnight.

The daily walks were not enough to win Cleveland's battle against increasing weight. Slowly he slipped past the 300-pound mark. And because he spent so little time outside, his skin turned a pasty white. Friends urged him to relax more, to find time to do more fishing.

But Cleveland would not take the time to relax. Running the city of Buffalo was an easy task compared to serving as governor of New York. He had known the people of Buffalo, from its famous and rich to its unknown and poor. He understood the city's needs. The state of New York was sprawling and diverse. Cleveland wanted to avoid making any mistakes.

Always a good judge of character, Cleveland picked his helpers carefully. Daniel Lamont proved an able secretary, willing to put in long hours and six-day weeks. Daniel Manning, the head of the state's Democratic Party, also offered vital support. "Don't expect special favors just because Grover's a Democrat," Manning warned party leaders. "We're all just people in his eyes, all just the same."

Among the Republicans, Cleveland was most impressed with a young man in the General Assembly named Theodore

Roosevelt. Young Roosevelt, like Cleveland, seemed eager to erase the shadows of corruption which had for so long loomed over politics.

Despite the help of friends and supporters, Cleveland continued to carry out the duties of his office by himself. He was not good at sharing responsibility. "The people voted for me," he told his friends, "and therefore *I* should serve them in every way I can." Often Cleveland worked himself to a state of near exhaustion. His personal goal was to rid the top of his desk of all paperwork. It never happened. Each morning there were documents and bills to study, sign, or veto.

Being Fair with the Fare

Cleveland vetoed many more bills than he signed. The state legislature swarmed with politicians representing special interests or businesses. "I've got a good nose for sniffing out the conniving sneaks who would pad their own pockets at the public's expense," Cleveland bragged. "If a bill does not benefit the people of this state and the state itself, I don't want it to cross my desk."

The Five-Cent Fare Bill posed special problems. New York City was tied together by an elevated railroad system largely controlled by financier Jay Gould. The crafty millionaire had made a large fortune by squeezing every penny he could out of the people who used the system. Recognizing Gould's greed and shady business dealings, legislators proposed that all fares on the transit system should be reduced to five cents. At certain times of the day, 10-cent fares would be charged. Gould fought the measure, arguing that he had a legal contract with the state. Few listened to his complaints, however.

Theodore Roosevelt helped lead the fight to reduce the

transit fare. "Some of this country's greatest thieves wear diamond stickpins and linen suits," Roosevelt charged. "They would rather watch people starve before tossing them a crumb." Politicians connected with Tammany Hall also called for the fare reduction. After the bill was passed by both the New York House of Representatives and the New York Senate, all that remained was for Governor Cleveland to sign it and it would become law.

The night he received the Five-Cent Fare Bill Cleveland sat at his desk for a long time. He read the proposal over and over. He rose and walked to the window. Most of Albany slept peacefully. Returning to his desk, Cleveland plopped into his chair and rubbed his thick neck. He knew the newspapers, the Democrats and Republicans, and, most important of all, the people would want him to sign this bill.

"No, I can't do it," Cleveland mumbled to himself. There was a principle involved, a question of right and wrong. Investors like Jay Gould had put up their money for the railroads when there was a major risk involved. Legal contracts had been signed. The investments had paid off richly. But was it fair to now change the contracts? No, not to Grover Cleveland it wasn't.

Cleveland was never one to avoid a fight. He took his veto directly to the legislators and explained why he could not sign the bill. He would probably end up being the most unpopular man in New York, he remarked.

Strangely, that never happened. The legislators realized that Cleveland was right. They had allowed their emotions to sway their judgment and common sense. The Five-Cent Fare Bill was an attempt to strike back at cruel and powerful men. Yet, it was not legal. Cleveland asked that people think with their conscience. It was what he always tried to do.

Quickly, Theodore Roosevelt and others spoke out

against the bill. Newspaper editors changed their opinions. Cleveland's actions once more won him wide support.

But there were two men who had little use for the governor of New York. One was State Senator Thomas Grady; the other was John "Honest John" Kelly. While the name of Grover Cleveland was praised in more and more homes across the state, Grady and Kelly plotted against New York's chief executive. Cleveland was a direct threat to all that Tammany Hall, their political base, stood for. Grady and Kelly were determined that no one man was going to change that.

Chapter 6
Fighting Tammany Hall

For almost 100 years, Tammany Hall had symbolized political power – specifically in New York City and generally throughout the state of New York. The name originated with the building in which the organization started meeting in 1789. Over the years, leaders of Tammany Hall had become adept at manipulating government money and jobs. There were few men like Grover Cleveland willing to challenge the corrupt system.

Thomas Grady was typical of those backed by Tammany Hall and sent to Albany. Young and brash, Grady displayed a smooth style with words and manners. He applied his eloquence to devious legislation often designed to divert tax money into Tammany Hall coffers. His wild drinking binges away from the Senate floor were known to many, yet the people from his district in New York City continued to elect him.

Overseeing Grady and other Tammany Hall political puppets was "Honest John" Kelly, who maintained Tammany operations in New York City. A good match for Grady as a manipulator, Kelly promised fame and fortune to men willing to follow orders and ask few questions. There were always a goodly number of volunteers.

Losing the Five-Cent Fare Bill was bitter medicine for the Tammany Hall organization, and they held Grover Cleveland responsible. Yet Grady wasted no time in rallying his troops behind the efforts of the Western Union Company to put its telegraph poles wherever it pleased across the state. "It is for the public good," Grady insisted. There was little secret that it was also for the "good" of Tammany Hall, because Western Union had promised sizable political contributions to those who would help in the venture.

Governor Cleveland, however, would have none of it. "Private corporations have no right to private property," he fired back as he vetoed the measure. "Let Western Union ask permission of landowners and pay them a fee. The state owes no favors to private companies. We have an obligation to protect our citizens."

POLITICAL BATTLEGROUNDS

Cleveland's interference infuriated Grady, who quickly called upon Kelly for support. The Tammany Hall chief traveled to Albany to meet with his loyal team players. Attention was soon to focus on a bill regarding immigrants, and a great deal of money and many jobs were involved. The Tammany Hall organization wanted nothing to stand in the way of the bill's passage, especially a 300-pound human obstruction named Cleveland.

When the Immigration Commission was established in 1882, it was intended to help those people from other countries who were pouring into New York City each day. The newcomers needed homes and jobs, for which the commissioners had a budget of $200,000. But little of the money ended up helping the immigrants. Instead, most of it was wasted by the commissioners. When a new bill appeared on Cleveland's desk—a bill designed to restructure the immigration program with a different set of commissioners—the governor signed it immediately. He then proposed William H. Murtha of Brooklyn to head the new commission.

"We'll decide who will head the commission!" Grady declared. "And we also have a list of 200 men we want named as harbor masters!"

Tammany Hall had issued a challenge and the fiesty governor accepted it. He refused to withdraw Murtha as his recommendation to head the new Immigration Commission. He also refused to appoint any of the men Grady wanted as harbor masters. "He'll give in," Kelly told his people in the state Senate. "Some men need a little time. Cleveland is a tough customer, but I don't think he's a fool."

However, Kelly proved to be a poor judge of character and a worse predictor of events. Furious at their failure to confirm Murtha, Cleveland wrote an angry letter to the state senators. He traced the sad treatment of immigrants, the waste of funds, and the reasons for Murtha being a fine choice to head the new organization. He accused the senators of being irresponsible, reminding them that they would have to answer to the people.

The letter had a major effect. Many senators wanted to approve Murtha. However, Grady still spoke against the choice and blocked action on the nomination. An outraged Cleveland then stood firm against the Tammany Hall selections for harbor masters.

"It's all-our war between Governor Cleveland and Tammany Hall," wrote one newspaper editor. "It is impossible to know which will be the first to give in. Certainly the Tammany machinery has squashed many a crusading politician in the past. But Grover Cleveland is a mighty big obstacle."

In the fall of 1883, Grover Cleveland took a political gamble. He wrote a personal letter to "Honest John" Kelly stating that he did not want Thomas Grady returned to the state Senate in the next election. It was a risky move, because Cleveland knew Kelly would probably make the letter public. And Kelly did just that. He hoped people would resent a governor telling them how to vote. But Kelly's actions backfired. He had greatly underestimated Cleveland's influence with the citizens of New York. When the senatorial elections were held in November of 1883, Thomas Grady was defeated.

The Democrats in New York paid a price for their internal squabbling, however. Republicans were elected to many seats in both the state Assembly and the Senate. That set the stage for a unique partnership between two men of different parties. The Democratic governor, Grover Cleveland, found an ally in the leader of the Republican Assembly, Theodore Roosevelt. Both men recognized the need for government free from any corrupt influence. Together, they worked to establish a civil service system in the state of New York that hired people based on ability rather than patronage.

SURGING TO THE TOP

By the time the Democrats held their national convention in Chicago in 1884, stories of the fighting governor of New York had traveled widely among the delegates. He was heralded as a champion of people's rights, a crusader against corruption, "The man who took on Tammany Hall—and won!" True, Grover Cleveland had been in the political spotlight for only a short time. But many people had had enough of Civil War generals and familiar names. There was an excitement to a new face and a scrapper in the political arena. Cleveland had challenged the leaders of powerful forces, and when need be, the people too. Few had forgotten how he had stood alone in the Five-Cent Fare controversy.

Before the Democrats gathered, the Republicans selected their candidate for President. Their choice was James Blaine, a former senator from Maine and the secretary of state under

President James Garfield. Like so many politicians of the time, Blaine was tainted with corruption from a railroad scheme that allowed him private gain while he was serving in office. Yet his name was well known and he would attract votes from all sections of the country.

Tammany Hall leaders tried hard to block Cleveland. "Anybody but Cleveland!" Grady and Kelly declared to the delegates arriving in Chicago. They attempted to paint the New York governor as a notorious drunk and a total incompetent. The slanderers found few believers, however.

Support continued to grow for Cleveland. Desperately, Grady and Kelly tried to rally backing for Thomas A. Hendricks, a little-known figure from Indiana who had received one vote in the first round of voting. Governor Benjamin Butler of Massachusetts joined the Tammany forces behind Hendricks in hopes the convention would become deadlocked. Butler harbored hopes that he might then become the presidential candidate.

The Tammany Hall plan was weak and made little headway. Because most of the delegates knew the Tammany team was out to destroy Cleveland, they gave Grady and Kelly no support. Sensing that his efforts were failing, Grady resorted to loud name-calling on the convention floor. "Cleveland is worthless," he shouted to anyone who would listen. "He's a drunk, a buffoon!"

Coming from Grady, the charges against Cleveland were totally ridiculous. Few at the convention were more widely known for wild drinking sprees. His voice was drowned out in a sea of boos. In contrast was the applause that greeted Edward Bragg of Wisconsin. Speaking on behalf of the supporters for Cleveland, Bragg bellowed, "They love Cleveland for his character!" Casting a scornful look at the Tammany crowd, Bragg continued, "But they also love him for the enemies he has made."

Momentum for the Cleveland nomination swept the con-

"WE LOVE HIM MOST FOR THE ENEMIES THAT HE HAS MADE."

As a presidential candidate in 1884, Cleveland's followers flaunted his image as a clean, untainted leader. "We love him most for the enemies that he has made" was a popular saying during the campaign. (Library of Congress.)

vention. A planned outburst for Hendricks failed. Once again, the Tammany Hall leadership suffered bitter embarrassment. By the second ballot, Cleveland was easily the winner.

A Dirty Campaign

The 1884 campaign was not one of issues. Rather, it was an examination of character. Both the public and private lives of Blaine and Cleveland fell open to inspection.

Blaine was severely attacked for decisions he made while in office. Again and again, he had voted for railroad expansion and land acquisition. Although he argued that he had personally believed in the railroad system, the fact that he had bought significant amounts of railroad stock hinted of less than honest dealing. The Democrats spread the possible scandal with a rhyming jingle:

> Blaine, Blaine, James G. Blaine,
> The continental liar
> From the state of Maine.

While the Democrats were attacking Blaine for public misdoings, the Republicans were holding Cleveland up to ridicule for private missteps. He was labeled "The Buffalo Hangman" for the executions he carried out while serving as sheriff of Erie County. Some called him "coward" for buying a substitute in the Civil War. Most of the accusations, however, were based on his relationship with Maria Halpin. It was an incident that Cleveland felt had no place in a political campaign. But rather than defend himself as Blaine constantly tried to do, Cleveland openly admitted the charges. He told his advisors, "Whatever you do, tell the truth." These instructions became known to voters across the country, and people gained even greater respect for the Democratic candidate.

As the campaign wound down, Blaine stumbled badly. A group of Protestant clergymen greeted him as he returned from a trip west. One of the greeters publicly labeled the Democrats as the party of "rum, Romanism and rebellion." The "rum" referred to Cleveland's personal drinking habits. The "Romanism" was an effort to alienate Irish Catholics, while the "rebellion" harkened back to Democratic opposition to the Civil War. However, rather than gain support for Blaine, the phrase became an ugly slur which united Democrats. Although he had not spoken the phrase himself, Blaine did not refute it.

Adding insult to injury, Blaine chose to attend a grand dinner party aimed at raising campaign funds. "For Millionaires Only" screamed newspaper headlines about the affair, which associated the Republican presidential candidate with John Jacob Astor, Jay Gould, and other business magnates. Democrats used the event to emphasize that Blaine's interests rested with the rich and powerful while Cleveland represented the common man.

Republicans hoped for sunny weather on election day because the farm population seemed to be leaning toward Blaine. But due to storms that dotted the country, the rural vote totals were low. The results came in slowly, but based on early reports, the *New York Tribune* boldly announced Blaine's election. Cleveland shrugged off the news. "I do believe the *Tribune* is a mite Republican," he said, "and perhaps more than a mite premature." Cleveland's remarks proved well founded. It took three days before all the votes were counted. But when they were, Grover Cleveland had squeaked by James G. Blaine, 4,874,986 to 4,851,981.

Chapter 7

Riding a Rollercoaster

Few men have ever been so unprepared for the job as was Grover Cleveland when he was inaugurated as President of the United States on March 4, 1885. Only four years before he had just been an ordinary attorney, handling routine legal matters in Buffalo. It seemed so strange that he was now the President. It was as though some raging and wild political tornado had swooped down and carried Cleveland through an amazing series of whirlwinds, then set him before a solemn Chief Justice of the Supreme Court, who administered the oath of office.

"It is as if fate and destiny formed a partnership," the new President wrote to a friend weeks after being sworn in. "I have done so little to merit so awesome a responsibility. May God grant me the power to carry out my duties."

NEW CHALLENGES, OLD ENEMIES

If the newly inaugurated Cleveland had hoped for a brief period of relief from pressure, as is usually accorded newly elected Presidents, he was in for a big disappointment. For more than 20 years, the Republicans had controlled the executive office, constantly adding members of their own

The formidable Cleveland was one to stand out in any crowd – this one being the spectators gathered for his first presidential inauguration on March 4, 1885. (Library of Congress.)

political party to government payrolls. The patronage system flourished like never before. Although the Civil Service Law of 1883 provided some protection for those government employees who were skilled in their jobs, the jobs of more than 100,000 federal workers still depended on the whims of bureaucratic chieftains of the political party in power.

Cleveland had publicly announced his support for the Civil Service Law, but leaders of the Democratic Party were convinced that they could change his mind. However, the new President served notice early in his administration that only the most partisan Republicans would be tossed out of their positions. He also said that Democrats as well as Republicans would be looking for new jobs if they lacked the ability to perform their duties. Cleveland's warnings did little to slow the stream of Democratic job-seekers. Even Wilson Bissell, Cleveland's law partner and friend in Buffalo, sought an appointment to the Cabinet or as an ambassador to some foreign country. When neither position was offered, Bissell turned against Cleveland, even refusing to speak to his former colleague.

Bissell's anger and frustration were matched by that of "Honest John" Kelly, who only under great pressure had thrown the Tammany Hall machinery behind Cleveland during the presidential contest. "You owe me," Kelly told Cleveland, and the Tammany boss would settle for nothing less than personally selecting a replacement for Henry G. Pearson, the Republican serving as postmaster of New York City. The postmaster's job was a rich political plum, carrying with it a large number of patronage positions.

Once again, Cleveland would not bend to the demands of "Honest John," and reappointed Pearson as postmaster. "I don't care what party he supports," Cleveland declared, "or what party supports him. Pearson is doing the job right and that's all that matters. Now, you can take him or leave him, but if you don't take him, the people will know why because I'll tell them." Although "Honest John" fought the reappointment, he could not muster enough support and Pearson held his position.

Unfinished Wars

Ever since the Civil War ended in 1865, relationships between northern and southern leaders had been strained. Wounds were slow to mend following the conflict, which had torn the states apart. In an effort to repair some of the damage, Cleveland named two former Confederate soldiers to his Cabinet.

The appointments were not simply tokens; indeed, it was never the chief executive's position that unqualified persons receive jobs. Nonetheless, it was an obvious attempt to bring the South back into the Union through a friendly, even gracious act.

"Token appointments!" one southern Democratic leader stormed. "We want more. Let us select our own people and then ask the noble Mr. Cleveland for his confirmation." The President, of course, would have none of such an arrangement. "I said it before my election, I said it in my inaugural address, and I shall say it forever—I shall select men who have merit and competency to fulfill the jobs given." The controversy continued, leading Cleveland to label the entire task of job appointments "a nightmare."

Republican newspapers across the country held the President accountable for any charges made against Republican office holders. At the same time, Democratic newspapers scolded him for not appointing members of his own party to federal positions. These journalistic attacks led Cleveland to lash out against his critics in the press. "I don't think there ever was a time when newspaper lying was so general and mean as the present, and there never was a country under the sun where it flourished as it does in this," said the President.

When the squabbling between Cleveland and the press faded to a minor roar, still another controversial issue raised its head. Cleveland's predecessor, Chester A. Arthur, had announced the opening of the Indian Territory for settlement. This land, now known as Oklahoma, had been promised to the Indians of the region. Cleveland, however, decided to honor the promise and closed the territory to settlers. He issued a firm warning that any intruders would be dealt with.

Again Cleveland faced assault on two sides. On one side were those who wanted to develop the Indian Territory. Many of these people were rich and powerful businessmen who hoped to enlarge their fortunes. They claimed that Cleveland had no right to take back what another President had decreed. On the other side, Apache and Ute tribes in the West demanded even more lands, and Cleveland was forced to dispatch federal troops to quell Indian uprisings.

Confiding to his sister Rose, who had come to Washington to serve as her brother's hostess in the White House, the weary Cleveland said, "You're the only appointment and decision I've made so far that I haven't had an argument about."

Philosophy of a President

One of Cleveland's major concerns was the financial stability of the nation. Enjoying a period of economic prosperity that provided the federal treasury with $70 million more than the government needed to meet its annual expenses, Cleveland advocated lowering tariffs. Not doing so, he said, would simply cause lawmakers to pass money-wasting laws. "Give a man a few extra dollars," noted Cleveland, "and he will spend what he does not need foolishly. Our Congress is no different."

A bachelor when he was first elected President, Cleveland called upon his younger sister, Rose Elizabeth, to act as the official White House hostess. (Library of Congress.)

The President also warned that the nation's fiscal system was in danger due to the hoarding of gold and coinage of silver dollars.

After saying what he had to say, Cleveland then retreated to the White House. There would be no arm twisting by or promises from this chief executive. Cleveland had a most conservative interpretation of presidential duties and responsibilities. Few men occupying the nation's top office have held such a narrow understanding of the role of the presidency. Cleveland realized that it was his responsibility to cast the spotlight on major matters of national concern, even suggesting possible solutions. But once he had spoken as chief executive, he quickly withdrew from the scene, clearly demonstrating his belief that legislative powers rested with Congress alone.

If there was one executive privilege Cleveland exercised with regularity (and often with a considerable amount of joy), it was the power to veto bills passed by Congress. He came to the presidency well trained in vetoing bills; it was a familiar task for him both as mayor of Buffalo and governor of New York.

This was a period in American history when elected officials were often dependent upon funds from special interest groups, such as big business. Therefore, many bills clearly benefiting industrial giants were swiftly passed by Congress. A reporter once asked Cleveland how he was so astute at spotting those bills obviously aimed at expanding the pocketbooks and extending the power of special interest groups. "I've been a fisherman a good many years," the President replied. "Bad bills and dead gills have a similar smell to them."

During his first term in office, Cleveland vetoed some 304 "bad bills," compared to a total of 132 bills vetoed by the previous 21 Presidents. "I promised the American people honesty and reform when I took the presidential oath," Cleveland declared, "and to allow such bills to become laws would be a violation of my duties."

Pensions and Politics

Among the most delicate problems facing Cleveland was the Civil War pension system. Created in 1862, during the term of President Abraham Lincoln, almost 900,000 pension claims had been filed by the time Cleveland took office. Over one-third had been approved, and those disapproved could be brought before Congress by individual legislators.

Pension claims were seldom investigated. After being processed by government clerks, claims were then passed by general consent of the Senate, with no quorum being required. On some "pension days," several hundred claims would be passed, many of them filed by former soldiers who had fictional injuries and terms of duties.

Cleveland ordered reviews of individual claims and vetoed many. The Grand Army of the Republic, representing Civil War veterans, and one of the most powerful pressure groups in the nation, attacked Cleveland and pushed Congress into adopting an even wider-ranging bill, the Dependent Pensions Act of 1887. "Veto this," warned GAR officials, "and we'll never forget it." Undaunted, Cleveland did exactly that. It was an action that would hurt him when he ran for re-election.

Much of the constant confrontation between the legislative and executive branches was the result of having a Republican-dominated Senate and a Democratic President. The Republican senators had controlled the Senate for almost 20 years, and they had little wish to relinquish any of the powers they had gained in that time.

Despite the fact that the majority of the nation's newspapers were in the hands of Republicans who led frequent attacks against Cleveland, the people maintained their support for their chief executive. It was a unique charisma that Cleveland possessed, for he was hardly a dashing, trim figure. During his first administration, he found his weight pushing 300 pounds. His balding head, accented by thick walrus-like whiskers, rested on a short neck that dissolved rapidly into corpulent shoulders and chest. "Rather dull and unimaginative," summed up one newspaper editor when asked to describe the American President by a foreign correspondent, "but his appearance is a delight for our political cartoonists."

A WHITE HOUSE FIRST

If there was one event during Cleveland's first administration that pulled both the people and news media together, it was the chief executive's marriage. Only James Buchanan, who had served as President from 1857 until 1861, had also entered the White House as a bachelor, and he had been 65 years old at the time. Cleveland, on the other hand, was only 47 upon taking the oath of office.

Frequent visits to the White House by Mrs. Emma Folsom, the widow of Cleveland's former law partner in Buffalo, caused rumors to filter through Washington that the President might be looking for a wife. Few paid attention to Mrs. Folsom's 21-year-old daughter, Frances, and the public announcement on May 28, 1886, of her engagement to the President caught most people by surprise. A graduate of Wells College in Aurora, New York, Frances found herself swept up in crowds of well-wishers. The wedding was held in the Blue Room of the White House on June 2, 1886, with only a few family members and close friends attending.

The President attempted to be as cordial as possible to members of the press, but Cleveland felt that a honeymoon was a private matter and that reporters had no business follow-

On June 2, 1886, Grover Cleveland and Frances Folsom were married in the Blue Room of the White House. (Library of Congress.)

*At age 21, Frances Folsom Cleveland became the youngest
First Lady in American history.* (Library of Congress.)

Thomas Nast: The Art of Politics

During his two terms as President of the United States, Grover Cleveland maintained a love-hate relationship with the press. In a time before television, radio, and movies, newspapers wielded maximum power and influence. ''There is nothing more valuable to our reading public in America than a good reporter,'' Cleveland declared. ''It's a shame there aren't more of them.''

There was, however, one individual in the world of journalism who Cleveland and millions of other Americans greatly appreciated. He was Thomas Nast, whose work lives on even today.

No master with words, Nast was a German immigrant whose cartoons and caricatures filled the pages of *Harper's Weekly* and eventually his own *Illustrated Almanac*. The Republican elephant? That is a Nast creation. So is the famed Democratic donkey. Nast was also the first artist to depict Santa Claus as a fat and jolly old man with snowy white whiskers.

Born September 27, 1840, in Landau, Germany, Nast was only six years old when his mother brought him to the United States. They settled in New York City, where his artistic talent blossomed early. He studied at the Academy of Design and was hired, at age 15, to draw for Frank Leslie's *Illustrated Weekly*. He became a full-time artist for *Harper's Weekly* in 1862, specializing in political cartoons and Civil War illustrations.

His work won the attention of President Abraham Lincoln, who called Nast ''our best recruiting sergeant'' because of his pictures poking fun at those northerners who opposed the war effort.

Nast's cartoons dotted the pages of *Harper's Weekly* for the next 25 years. A favorite target during the late 1860s was the political machinery of the notorious William M. Tweed of Tammany Hall. While Cleveland challenged the devious operations of Tammany Hall in words, Nast ridiculed the organization in drawings. The campaign against Tammany Hall waged by *Harper's Weekly* and other publications eventually forced Boss Tweed to flee to Europe in order to avoid arrest. However, because Nast's caricatures were carried around the world, Tweed was discovered hiding out in Spain in 1876.

For the most part, Nast seemed to appreciate the presidential efforts of Grover Cleveland. More than once, however, the chief executive found himself wincing from a critical cartoon. ''I'd rather be attacked in words by ten editors,'' said Cleveland, ''than be the victim of one Nast drawing.''

During the 1870s and 1880s, Nast illustrated for many periodicals. He also developed a popular lecture tour in which he sketched as he spoke. The crowds enjoyed every presentation, applauding both his nimble fingers and his quick wit. After he resigned from *Harper's Weekly* in 1886, he began publishing his own magazine, *Nast's Illustrated Almanac*.

Early in 1902, President Theodore Roosevelt appointed Nast consul general at Guayaquil, Ecuador. Shortly after beginning his official duties, the famed cartoonist took ill. Nast died in Guayaquil on December 7, 1902.

ing the newly married couple to their retreat in the Maryland mountains. Nonetheless, resourceful and overly zealous reporters tracked down the honeymooners, further aggravating Cleveland and sharpening the battle between himself and the press.

Throughout her seven years as First Lady, Frances Cleveland strove to maintain some privacy for her husband and their family. Her efforts seldom succeeded, leading President Cleveland to nickname reporters "the ghouls of the press."

Back to Business

Cleveland was not one to stay away from his presidential desk for long. Returning to Washington after his honeymoon, he dug into his duties with new vigor and dedication.

A top priority was his personal concern for the country's economic stability. Although never formally educated in business and having little business experience, other than past legal associations with business clients, Cleveland nevertheless possessed an acute sense of economics. He recognized the importance of workable relationships between labor and management, encouraging both workers and owners to peacefully negotiate salaries and working conditions.

The countless railroad strikes that occurred in 1886 were

a personal disappointment to Cleveland as well as a potential threat to the nation's economic stability. He thereupon urged Congress to establish a special labor commission to mediate labor-management disagreements. That request was spotlighted by a violent confrontation between police and workers in Chicago. The Haymarket Riot, as the clash came to be known, resulted in seven deaths and 50 people injured. It influenced Congress to pass legislation leading to the creation of the Department of Labor.

Railroads again captured Cleveland's attention in 1887. For years, railroad owners had been laying tracks crisscrossing the country, grabbing lands as they could and setting freight prices as they wished. The power to bring life or death to a company or community often rested with a railroad owner. It was hardly a satisfying economic standard, as Cleveland well knew, and yet there was little that could be done.

The rail industry had managed to outmaneuver efforts of individual states to exercise some degree of control. However, with the passage in 1887 of the Interstate Commerce Act by Congress, railway magnates found their powers reduced and new regulations enforced. Cleveland signed the act immediately, then issued executive orders to retrieve over 80 million acres of public land grants from railroad owners and cattle ranchers.

By late 1887, Cleveland's attentions again focused on the United States Treasury. Money continued to swell the nation's coffers, causing the legislators to toss around wild ideas as to how it might be spent. "Divide the surplus among the men in the country," one senator suggested. (It was far too early for women to be considered in such matters.) Another senator thought building free luxury resorts across the country would be a suitable idea for the extra revenue. To Cleveland, the only valid proposal was to reduce tariffs. It became the major focus of his dealings with the Congress.

Unfortunately, he offered no specifics, no details. "Why

not present them with the kind of measure you think appropriate?" one aide offered. "That's not the President's job," Cleveland snapped. Because the President failed to exert more definitive leadership on the tariff issue, he did little to help reduce the bulging national treasury. It was fateful timing for such inaction, for Americans were preparing to vote for the 23rd President of the United States. The election promised to be a close one.

Chapter 8
Intermission

When the Democrats gathered in St. Louis for their national convention early in June 1888, there was little question as to whom their candidate for President would be. There was no doubt that Grover Cleveland had made enemies during his first term in office, particularly enemies in Tammany Hall and the Grand Army of the Republic. But Democratic leaders also knew that the man presently occupying the White House still enjoyed a warm relationship with the people of the nation. Allen G. Thurman, a former senator from Ohio, was tapped as his running mate.

It looked like it would be a rematch between President Cleveland and Republican challenger James G. Blaine. Blaine, however, declined the nomination. The Republican spotlight then shifted to Benjamin Harrison, a grandson of former President William Henry Harrison, who had served as a general in the Civil War and as a senator from Ohio. A quiet, lackluster figure, Harrison had displayed few signs of leadership. But the Republicans considered that an asset because there would then be less to criticize. Cleveland's record was the major issue.

A MEAN CAMPAIGN

The 1888 campaign had barely begun when ugly rumors started to sweep across the country. "It's said old Cleveland beats his wife," one fellow would declare. "It's not surprising," came the reply. "It's probably how the gruff, mean bear got her to marry him in the first place." Although the gossip was without foundation, the talk found eager listeners.

It was never a secret that Cleveland was a workaholic, and he demanded unlimited time and energy from his staff members as well. Newspaper cartoonists and reporters delighted in depicting the President as a cruel and unyielding man, hardly capable of offering any semblance of kindness and comfort to a girl young enough to be his daughter. Frances Folsom Cleveland was the media's sweetheart, while Grover Cleveland was their tyrannical target.

Adding to the injury caused by those who spread rumors were the efforts of Tammany Hall leaders. Cleveland had not played by their rules once too often, and they were determined to remove him from the White House. Although it was crucial for Cleveland to win the state of New York, he would not do a thing to enhance his status.

Rich American businessmen, many of them riding the wave of prosperity with the help of the high tariffs, poured money into Harrison's campaign. Chauncey Depew, head of the New York Central Railroad, declared, "The nation will fall on its face without the present tariffs. Any American voting for Cleveland is gambling with his job and his financial security."

Feeling it beneath the dignity of the office, Cleveland refused to campaign publicly for President. In contrast, Harrison gave almost 100 major addresses, most of them attacking Cleveland on the tariff position. The President fumed in the White House, declaring that industry owners would simply have to become more competitive pricewise if tariffs were lowered. However, when his advisors urged him to take his thoughts to the people, Cleveland vehemently refused. "But you're splitting our party and uniting the Republicans!" one aide asserted. "I'll not trade my standards for votes," Cleveland shot back.

"The Happiest Man"

In the November election, the count of popular votes was 5,540,309 for Cleveland and 5,444,337 for Harrison. But the Tammany Hall machinery in New York was well oiled, providing Harrison with a plurality of 13,000 votes in that state. This made the total electoral vote in Harrison's favor.

Despite his disappointment in losing, Cleveland expressed no regrets. On the contrary, he declared himself "the happiest man in the United States." His wife quietly told the White House staff to take good care of the furniture for she and Mr. Cleveland would be returning in four years. The servants chuckled good naturedly at the prediction, then realized that Frances Cleveland had not meant the remark as a joke.

In the waning months of his first term as President, Cleveland managed to raise a few diplomatic eyebrows. During the election campaign, Cleveland sent the British ambassador in Washington, Sir Lionel Sackville-West, back to England after the diplomat had been tricked and used by Republican politicians. Because no substitute was returned to Washington, the American ambassador in London appeared to be nothing more than a court jester. He asked Cleveland if he might return to the United States. Cleveland agreed, leaving the United States and Great Britain without ambassadors in each other's countries.

In yet another dramatic diplomatic episode, Cleveland came close to involving the nation in a war with Germany. The ever-expanding German influence in other countries, led

Frances Cleveland clearly found living at the White House comfortable and exciting. At the end of her husband's first term, she told the servants not to put anything away because they would be back. (Library of Congress.)

by Chancellor Bismarck, reached a head, as far as Cleveland was concerned, in Samoa. German authorities had gone so far as to exile King Malietoa and to install a man of their own choice as chief. Cleveland sent American warships to Samoa's capital of Apia, and Germany did the same. While each side waited for the other to make some mistake that would start an all-out conflict, Mother Nature stepped in. A vicious typhoon whirled across the Pacific, hurling the ships of both countries against sharp coral reefs. The disaster diverted attention from the diplomatic hostilities, and the tension eased.

New Roads

On March 4, 1889, Benjamin Harrison was inaugurated as 23rd President of the United States. The Clevelands headed to New York City, where Grover promptly joined the law firm of Bangs, Stetson, Tracy and McVeagh. Its offices were near Wall Street, to which Cleveland took a streetcar each day from his four-story home at 816 Madison Avenue.

For all his adult life, Cleveland had enjoyed fishing. He was delighted, therefore, when he found a cottage available for summer retreats in the Sippican Harbor area of Massachusetts. He and Frances named their vacation home Gray Gables.

Despite the slower pace and the pleasure of not having to constantly wrestle with major national problems, Cleveland found himself unable to enjoy life. Often, he simply shook his head at the Republican-controlled Congress and Republican President Harrison as they moved down a road Cleveland was certain spelled doom and destruction. As veterans' pensions were increased, new higher tariffs were imposed, and more silver was coined, each day seemed to bring the country closer to economic disaster.

Inwardly, Cleveland fought a constant battle over whether

The summer of 1892 found presidential incumbent Benjamin Harrison facing another challenge by Cleveland in a run for the White House. Many Americans favored protection of the country's businesses, as symbolized by Harrison in this cartoon, while Cleveland promoted free trade interests. (Library of Congress.)

or not to speak out about what was happening in Washington. As a former President, he felt such criticisms were improper. But finally, he could keep silent no longer. He argued publicly against the spending policies of the Republicans, issuing stern warnings against the dangers of the new high tariffs sponsored by Senator William McKinley as well as the inflationary coinage of silver.

Picking a Winner

In the congressional elections of 1890, almost half of the Republicans in the House of Representatives lost their seats to Democratic opponents. It was clear that the nation had had enough of Republicans' policies. The Democratic Party began to rebuild.

By the time the Democrats met in late June of 1892 to pick a Presidential candidate, Cleveland was the obvious choice. Nevertheless, Tammany Hall leaders tried to block his nomination. "If we don't want him in his home state, why should you?" challenged the Tammany delegates. The answer came back quickly: "Because he can win!" Again, the Republicans nominated Harrison, but there was little enthusiasm for the man some claimed could not even spell "leader," much less be one.

Neither Cleveland nor Harrison campaigned actively. But the election was given some spice by the nomination of General James B. Weaver of Iowa to run on the Populist Party ticket, which advocated free silver coinage, establishment of postal savings banks, and a graduated income tax. The Populists captured more than one million votes in the 1892 election, netting 22 electoral votes. Apparently, Weaver had taken votes away from the incumbent Harrison, allowing Cleveland to get 277 electoral votes to Harrison's 145. After a brief intermission, Grover Cleveland was headed back to the White House.

When Populism Was Popular

Democrat, Republican, Populist—what's that? What is a Populist? Certainly the question would not have been asked in the 1890s. If it was, President Grover Cleveland would have known the answer immediately.

The populism movement was a self-defense alliance started by farmers in the 1870s. Suffering from falling crop prices and higher operating costs, the people who tilled the soil in the Midwest, West, and South grouped together to fight the ever-rising freight rates charged by the railroads and the high interest rates charged by the banks. The farmers' alliances claimed to support the goals of the ''common people.'' The entire movement was called populism, and its backers were labeled Populists.

The major goals of populism were an increased money supply (more silver coinage), more government regulation of business, and anything else that would help farmers and general laborers in America. Because Grover Cleveland fought against increasing silver coinage and because he seemed to favor the barons of big business, especially the railroad leaders, he was often the political target of the Populists.

At a time in history when flamboyant Democrats and Republicans were relatively rare, the Populists boasted a wide variety of colorful eccentrics. There was Senator William Peffer, whose beard covered the better part of his chest, giving him a Rip Van

Winkle look. Peffer used his appearance ef-
fectively, particularly among those who expected him to be some kind of country
bumpkin, for he could speak with fire and
eloquence.

Another Populist, Congressman Jerry
Simpson, accused a Republican opponent he
was debating of being the ''type to wear silk
socks.'' Noting Simpson's homespun appearance, one reporter suggested that the
congressman himself probably wore no socks
at all. For the rest of his life, Simpson was
nicknamed ''Sockless Jerry.''

The Populists also had ardent female supporters. One such was Mary Elizabeth Lease,
who captured people's attention when she
urged farmers to raise ''less corn and more
Hell.'' Lease, called ''The Kansas pythoness,''
studied law after bringing up four children.
''Beware the Irishwoman with the tongue of
fire,'' opponents warned, and her fiery out-
bursts on many a stage justified the warning.

The farmers' alliances grew in number and
power. Finally, in 1891, delegates met in Cin-
cinnati, Ohio, and formed the Populist Party.
The following year, the Populists put up
James B. Weaver of Iowa for President and
James G. Field of Virginia for Vice-President.
Among other reforms, the party platform supported free silver and government ownership
of railroads as well as of telegraph and
telephone lines. Although Weaver and Field
lost, they tallied over one million votes,
enough to capture 22 electoral votes. In addi-

tion many Populist candidates won seats in Congress.

In 1896, the Populists put their support behind the Democratic candidate, William Jennings Bryan, for President. After he lost, there was a general movement away from the Populist goals that led to the party's decline by the early 1900s. Today, the term ''populist'' is used to identify any person who seems to represent the best interests of the farmer and common man.

Chapter 9
Back in Charge

There is no doubt that Grover Cleveland felt considerably more confident as he took the presidential oath of office on March 4, 1893, then he did exactly eight years before. It was equally doubtful that he anticipated the deluge of immediate problems he faced. Economic chaos reigned throughout the country. Banks were closing, businesses were failing, and people were losing their jobs. With Democrats controlling both houses of Congress and a Democratic President in the White House, the national spotlight focused on Cleveland trying to pull the country out of the growing depression.

As the newly installed President carefully surveyed the economic situation, the financial ship of state sank even further. In May the stock market collapsed, several giant companies declared bankruptcy, and the unrestricted coinage of silver continued unchecked. As if there were not enough national problems to deal with, Cleveland found himself wrestling with a medical problem that threatened his life – cancer of the mouth. Concerned about the effect an announcement of his cancer might have on the general public as well as on Congress, Cleveland decided to keep the information quiet. After calling a special congressional session for August, the President stole away to have surgery.

FIGHTING A DEPRESSION

Repeal of the Sherman Silver Purchase Act, which had been passed by Congress in 1890, during the Harrison administration, was a necessity if economic stability in the country was to be restored, according to Cleveland's thinking. But he hardly anticipated the bitter fighting that would break out before the act was repealed. In his own words, "The administration must be ready with some excellent substitute for the Sherman Act." However, when Congress looked to the President for a specific program, none was there. Cleveland knew exactly what he did not want, and he would not accept any compromise. Unfortunately, he lacked the resourcefulness to come up with any alternative.

If Cleveland had hoped for immediate positive results from the repeal of the Sherman Silver Purchase Act, he was sadly disappointed. The gold reserve in the United States Treasury continued to drop, causing Cleveland to order the sale of bonds. A nucleus of American bankers, headed by J. P. Morgan, gave their financial backing to three bond issues. That support caused concern among many citizens that the United States government was largely dependent, at least financially, on a small group of Wall Street bankers and businessmen. The depression that gripped the nation's economy was too complicated to be solved by any one presidential action.

Once again, as he had in his first administration, Cleveland tackled the tariff problem. If repealing the Sherman Silver Purchase Act did not put the nation's financial system on a stronger footing, surely reducing tariffs would. Many of the Democrats swept into office with Cleveland had promised to reduce taxes on imported goods. With a tariff bill put together by West Virginian William L. Wilson, the Democratic senators and representatives in Congress attempted to do just that. However, the reductions were considerably less than Cleveland wanted.

Wilson's bill passed the House with minor skirmishes, but a major battle took place in the Senate. The protectionists, those who feared opening the country's markets to a flood of foreign goods, began taking apart the tariff bill point by point.

Senator Arthur Gorman of Maryland, respected by both political parties, urged caution in passing any tariff measure that would negatively affect the nation's economic future. "Yes, we have an obligation to our own consciences," noted Gorman, "that we must honor the promises with which we ran and were elected. But if this country is to remain intact after we and the voters are long gone, we must exercise wisdom and care in every move we make." Following Gorman's advice, the senators added over 600 amendments to Wilson's initial bill. Cleveland fumed in the White House, totally exasperated over the Senate action.

When the final bill, known as the Wilson-Gorman Tariff of 1894, reached Cleveland's desk, he refused to sign it. It was far from the reform he wanted. Thus, the bill became law without presidential endorsement. Angrily, Cleveland dispatched a personal letter to the Senate, sharing his disappointment with their actions and noting that the Wilson-Gorman Tariff fell "far short of the consummation for which we have long labored."

Cleveland's words and feelings did little more than annoy the senators, many of whom had given in to his wishes about silver coinage. In their eyes, their leader always seemed to know what he did not want but he never seemed to offer a definite alternative. Both the senators and Cleveland were disgusted and frustrated, not the attitudes that would pull the country out of a depression.

OVERSEAS PROBLEMS

As if the domestic troubles plaguing the nation were not bad enough, Cleveland found himself in the midst of an incident beyond the country's boundaries. During President Harrison's administration, the American minister in Hawaii had thrown his personal support and the strength of the U. S. Marines behind a bloodless revolution leading to the overthrow of Queen Liliuokalani. A treaty of annexation was quickly put together and submitted to the United States Senate for ratifica-

Queen Liliuokalani of Hawaii proved to be one of several problems that Grover Cleveland faced during his second term in office. (Library of Congress.)

tion. The treaty was pending approval when Cleveland took office.

After withdrawing the document and investigating the matter personally, Cleveland concluded that the American minister had not acted honorably in the matter. Cleveland then asked Congress for help in restoring the queen to power. "America's honor is at stake," he declared.

Cleveland's actions were criticized by many congressmen as being against the best interests of the nation. "It was a perfect opportunity to expand the interest of the United States in the Pacific!" declared one senator, with others echoing similar sentiments.

Once more, the press denounced Cleveland's actions, but the chief executive would not bend. "Fortunately, an individual possesses a conscience," noted Cleveland, "a possession sadly lacking in the collective body of journalists across this great land." Queen Liliuokalani was not returned to power; instead, a provisional government was established. But Hawaii was not annexed to the United States.

Perhaps what angered so many American citizens about the Hawaiian affair was that their elected leader seemed to be out of step with the times. This was, after all, a period of "manifest destiny," a label suggesting that the United States had become and would remain a major force in world affairs. With such an understood prophecy, was it not appropriate to acquire new lands and extend the nation's influence internationally? There were countless Americans who believed exactly that, and it troubled them to see their leader unwilling to annex new lands wherever and whenever possible.

Trouble with England

If Cleveland slipped in the public's opinion because of the Hawaiian incident, his popularity took a great leap upward when he confronted England over a long-standing problem.

The trouble began over the boundary between Venezuela and British Guiana in South America. With American businessmen looking around the world for possible development and expansion, Cleveland felt he should take action. He suggested that the entire matter be submitted to arbitration because the boundary had been in dispute since 1814, when the British had first acquired three provinces of Dutch Guinea and turned them into an independently governed province.

Despite Cleveland's request, the British foreign office again seemed willing to set the matter aside. Furious with the dilly-dallying, Cleveland invoked the Monroe Doctrine by reminding the British of the document's opposition to European interference in the Western Hemisphere. Busy with critical disputes in South Africa and the Middle East, British leaders still chose to ignore Cleveland's request for arbitration regarding the South American boundary.

By the winter of 1895, Cleveland's patience ran out. He called upon the United States Congress to appoint a commission to investigate the matter and establish fair boundaries to settle the dispute. If England attempted to take any more land than designated, Cleveland asserted that the United States would "resist by every means in its power, as a willful aggression upon its rights and interests." Loosely translated, the words suggested that the nation would go to war. Immediately, Congress backed up Cleveland's action by appropriating $100,000 for the establishment of the boundary commission.

The leaders of the British government were stunned. A tone of reconciliation, concerned and friendly, set in at once, and boundary arbitration between Venezuela and British Guinea began immediately.

Beyond settling a boundary dispute between South American countries, the incident sent a message to the world that President Grover Cleveland could show a mighty hand when so moved and that his nation would play a key role in international relations. Involvement in, as opposed to isolation from, world affairs seemed to be the direction the United States was taking.

In the White House, Cleveland enjoyed a momentary period of satisfaction. But, as always, just over the horizon appeared new problems — problems that would test every skill and quality of character the President possessed.

Grover and Frances Cleveland relaxing at their New Jersey home in 1907 with their children (from left to right), Esther, Francis, Marion, and Richard. Their oldest daughter, Ruth, died in 1904. (Library of Congress.)

Chapter 10

Strikes and Struggle

As the public's evaluation of President Cleveland's performance in the White House bounced up and down, the people clearly enjoyed the activities of the First Family. Frances Folsom Cleveland brought a youthful excitement and elegance into the White House. Charming and tactful, she soon became a favorite of the American public. Despite the President's constant efforts to provide some privacy for those he loved most dearly, it was virtually impossible.

Grover and Frances Cleveland had obviously agreed to have a family. Whereas the couple may have thought such a decision was their own business, the American people felt they had a rightful share in the results of that decision. Although Cleveland's five children were not all born while he occupied the White House, the arrival of each new baby received much press attention. Daughter Ruth (for whom the "Baby Ruth" candy bar was named) was born on October 3, 1891. Esther arrived on September 9, 1893, and a third girl, Marion, was born July 7, 1895. The final two babies were boys—Richard arriving on October 28, 1897, and Francis, born on July 18, 1903. The Clevelands' first child, Ruth, died at the age of 12 of diptheria.

Cleveland welcomed the opportunity to spend time with his family, occasionally expressing feelings that he might have thought twice about seeking the pre~~~~~
he would eventually be s~~~~

of this position are awesome," he moaned at times. "To live with a President is to live with a monster."

UNHAPPY VOICES

As Cleveland grumbled over presidential responsibilities, another kind of complaining was sweeping the country. By 1894, over four million Americans, out of a population of 65 million, were unemployed. Those without jobs had little sympathy for a chief executive surrounded by servants in Washington. Indeed, newspaper pictures of the smiling and portly Cleveland served only as reminders to many of their downtrodden circumstances.

In the spring of 1894, an "army" of several hundred poor and unemployed marched on the nation's capital from Massillon, Ohio. Led by "General" Jacob S. Coxey, the marchers hoped to get Congress to pass a multimillion-dollar bill to build roads, thus offering jobs to the unemployed. "We are not begging or asking for money," Coxey asserted. "We want work." Cleveland was unimpressed, ordering his subordinates to reject any petition or requests offered by the marchers. Coxey was arrested and sent to jail for 20 days for trespassing on White House grounds.

The Pullman Strike

On the heels of the Coxey march came an even greater labor confrontation, this one in Pullman, Illinois. The entire town was owned by the Pullman Palace Car Company, which rented houses to employees. The model community, just outside Chicago, fared well as the Pullman Company gradually became the leader in manufacturing luxury railroad sleeping cars. But when business fell off during the depression, wages were reduced 25 percent. However, when investors received a seven percent dividend, company workers grumbled.

Despite the 25 percent reduction in their wages, the rent for housing remained the same. Seeking advice from the American Railway Union, Pullman employees were told to negotiate for higher wages or lower rents. George Pullman, owner of the company, would grant neither. And although he had promised no reprisals against the spokesmen of the workers' union, three were immediately discharged. The entire union membership then went out on strike, causing the company to close its doors.

The leader of the American Railway Union, Eugene Debs, feared violence if the matter could not be settled quickly. "We must always be willing to talk," Debs affirmed at the union's national convention, and encouraged Pullman officials to open lines of communication. When Pullman leaders refused to negotiate, the union voted to boycott—stop servicing—all Pullman cars in the nation. This involved 23 railroads operating in 27 states. More importantly, the boycott pitted the American Railway Union against the General Managers Association, an organization that would listen to no labor spokespeople.

Despite Debs' efforts to maintain a peaceful tone, members of his union heaped verbal abuse on train crews, leading thousands of additional workers to walk off their jobs. Across the Midwest, travel by rail slowed to a standstill. The *Chicago Tribune* reported that citizens were "terrorized," with Debs coordinating looting and rioting.

Attorney General Richard Olney, formerly an attorney for the railroads, urged federal action. He demanded that Cleveland send troops to quell the striking workers. "The railways carry the United States mail," Olney argued, "and any interference with the mails is a federal offense."

Illinois Governor John P. Altgeld insisted that the state could deal with the Pullman situation, that newspaper accounts were exaggerated, and that no federal troops were needed. Having had more than his share of newspaper sensationalism, Cleveland chose not to take action immediately. "Reporters are quick to turn an argument into a brawl," Cleveland told his advisors. "Anything to please their editors and sell newspapers."

While the chief executive chose not to get involved, Olney took an opposite course. He spearheaded a drive leading to a legal order against the workers, claiming the mail service was being disrupted. What had started as employees seeking negotiation with their employer now became a situation where the employees were opposing the United States government. Headlines in the *Chicago Tribune* during late June of 1894 screamed of Debs as being a "dictator" and claimed "Mobs Bent on Ruin!" Other newspapers picked up the tone of the events rather than the facts. As he read accounts of the Pullman incidents, Cleveland's concern grew. Olney's voice heightened the chief executive's agitation.

Forceful Resolution

Olney dispatched 4,000 United States marshals to railroad staging areas to make sure the mails were kept moving. He appointed Edwin Walker as a special U.S. attorney to plea for an injunction against the strikers. (It was hardly a wise choice because Walker was an attorney for the Milwaukee Road, one of the railroads directly involved.)

Further fanning the flames, Olney shared with the newspapers a telegram sent from his Chicago office claiming that the city was practically under mob control. The telegram was the final straw for Cleveland. As President, he felt responsible for maintaining law and order, continuing interstate transportation, and delivering the United States mails. Federal troops were ordered to Chicago to establish and maintain martial law.

Union workers had, indeed, caused damage. Even Eugene Debs, who was opposed to violence, was speaking openly of "civil war" to bring about a proper resolution. Then, with the arrival of federal troops, open conflict broke out and seven men were killed on July 7.

The bloodshed led to the immediate arrest of Debs for obstructing the United States mail. Cleveland outlawed organized assemblies, thus preventing people from attending meetings. Although Governor Altgeld attempted to offer advice, Cleveland would have none of it. With a legal order preventing them from stopping trains or interfering with the mail, and with their union leaders in jail, the Pullman workers gave up their strike.

A later investigation ordered by Cleveland concluded that the Pullman Company had acted in a dictatorial manner without regard for humane considerations and that union workers had broken the law. The American labor movement took a giant step backward, while the verdict on Cleveland's actions was mixed. Some felt he had little choice, based on what he was told or what he had read. Others felt he had asserted federal force in areas covered by states' rights. Altgeld firmly maintained that Cleveland had insulted the people by ignoring local government, and that the President was "in violation of a basic principle of our institutions." Reaffirming his intentions only to do what *had* to be done, Cleveland declared the "entire Pullman affair closed."

THE PAIN OF POLITICS

To a vast number of Americans, Grover Cleveland seemed to have been around for a long time. As his second term in office reached its midway point, there were many grumblings about "that big man in the White House who's been there forever." Harrison's single term had barely been noticed; Benjamin Harrison had slipped rapidly into obscurity by returning to Indiana, out of the public eye.

Everything Cleveland tried to curb the continuing economic depression did not work. Sadly, his creative ideas were few. He was against increased silver coinage, high tariffs, and imperialistic expansion into other countries. Always, he seemed to be *against* attitudes or programs set before him. Seldom, if ever, did he initiate ideas. "He certainly knows how to veto a bill," observed one longtime Congressman, "but I doubt if he'd know how to write one himself."

By contrast, the Republican Party had more than its share of flamboyant characters. Gentle but sharp spoken, looking like he was molded to be a President, Senator William McKinley of Ohio commanded a sense of awed respect when he spoke. His strong defense of the tariff as "the foundation of the nation's growth and the protective covering for wage earners" constantly thwarted Cleveland's attempts to bring the country's economy back to life. "That McKinley Tariff has been with us for over five years," Cleveland huffed in 1895, "and we're still trying to pull ourselves out of a depression. Can't the people see a high tariff is not the answer to our financial problems?" Apparently, they could not. McKinley enjoyed an ever-rising popularity.

Exhibiting a contrasting style was fellow Republican Theodore "Teddy" Roosevelt. Americans took readily to the witty and smiling fellow who seemed to prefer punching cows out west to exchanging society gossip among his wealthy friends on the east coast. A bundle of energy, Teddy Roosevelt brought new life to the political arena, forever coining catchy phrases to replace the tired labels of government. Cleveland had watched and even admired Roosevelt's astute performance when both were officials in New York state. But now, as Cleveland found his staid and somber approach toward leadership under frequent attack from the nimble-mouthed Roosevelt, the President more than once felt hurt by his respected rival.

Riding the Two-Wheeler

During the first term of President Grover Cleveland (1885–1889), few Americans knew the difference between a spoke and a handlebar (other than the latter referred to a full mustache). But by the time the honorable Mr. Cleveland returned for his second stay at the White House (1893–1897), bicycles dotted every city street and country road. Although there is no proof that Cleveland himself ever boarded a two-wheeler for a spin around Washington, there is ample evidence that his trim, attractive First Lady kept a bicycle in the executive mansion. Their first born, Baby Ruth as she was affectionately nicknamed by the public and a candy bar producer, had a special miniature model sent to her.

It is impossible to know exactly what caused Americans to jump on the wagon, or, in this case, a bicycle, and peddle an eccentric little vehicle into a recreational activity called "the most spectacular craze of all." Certainly, bicycling was not new to the country, but it was not until the design was streamlined to satisfy all shapes and sizes of riders that the bike caught on. The development of the pneumatic tire helped, too.

The popularity of bicycling skyrocketed when the general public learned it was the "in thing" among celebrities. Why, even Lillian Russell, the great actress and singer, rode her bicycle daily in New York City's Central Park. This was just her regular machine, however. The jewel-studded, golden model presented to her by longtime admirer Diamond Jim Brady was kept in a leather case. (Brady supposedly had a collection of a dozen golden bicycles for himself.)

Eugene Sandow, known across America as "The Monarch of Muscle," recommended bicycling as fine exercise, causing countless American males who envied Sandow's trim physique to take up a regular regimen of peddling. A dazzling London actress, Anna Held, delighted reporters when she rode a bike off her passenger ship upon arriving at New York City. The shapely and lovely Miss Held displayed both her impressive singing voice and gymnastic skills as she captured the attention of those on the dock.

Bicycling soon became a serious sport as well as a recreational pastime. For women, it was even more. Not only did it provide healthy exercise, bicycling also offered an opportunity for new fashion. Hems were raised and female outfits became less rigid and confining. Although males were allowed the freedom to mount and dismount in any way, an entire set of ladylike manners were devised for all activities while "cycling."

Sunday was the favorite day for bicycling, replacing the customary walk with the family. Preachers ranted and raved against the evils of bicycling on the Sabbath ("You cannot serve God and skylark on a bicycle"), but people rode nonetheless.

As the 19th century came to an end, the

craze that was bicycling dissolved into an accepted phase of family life, a mode of transportation falling somewhere between the tricycle and the automobile. It is estimated that today a bicycle can be found in one out of every three garages in the nation.

Internal Strife

Although Cleveland felt the pains of critical comment by leaders of the Republican Party, the sting was even greater from critics within the Democratic Party. Among the loudest and most frequent of Democratic critics was William Jennings Bryan from Nebraska.

Cleveland remembered that he had barely unpacked his bags in the White House when the open-handed Bryan came begging for patronage jobs to hand to his associates back home. Perfecting his skills as a public speaker, Bryan swiftly climbed the Democratic political ladder, largely through harsh criticisms of the man in the White House. While Cleveland fought to maintain the gold standard, Bryan advocated free silver coinage. As Cleveland desperately tried to pull the country out of the economic depression by enlisting the help of major businessmen, Bryan demanded strict business and railroad controls.

As Democratic leaders around the nation began early preparations for the presidential contest of 1896, it was obviously going to be a battle between those favoring "Clevelandism" and those supporting "Bryanism." Of the two potential candidates, Cleveland was adamant about not accepting a third term under any circumstances. On the other hand, Bryan was almost drooling openly for the opportunity to run.

While Cleveland was wrapped up with day-to-day matters as President, Bryan skillfully put together a strong group of supporters to take with him to the Democratic convention in Chicago. Most responsive to Bryan were the silver supporters of the West, Midwest, and South.

Meeting in St. Louis just before the Democratic convention, the Republicans announced their support of a gold standard on which to maintain a sound currency. They then nominated William McKinley and Garret Hobart as their candidates for President and Vice-President.

The politically astute Cleveland was convinced the Republicans had made wise decisions, especially in their support of the gold standard. He hoped the Democrats would do the same, but it would not be their President who would try to influence them. On July 1, 1896, Cleveland headed for a vacation at Sippican Harbor. Whatever the Democrats did in Chicago, they would do it without his advice or presence.

"A Cross of Gold"

What the Democratic delegates did was according to plan — the plan of William Jennings Bryan. The silver supporters got their plank written into the party platform, its policy statement. William Jennings Bryan boldly told the delegates, "You shall not press down upon the brow of labor this crown of thorns. You shall not sacrifice mankind upon a cross of gold." Truly, Bryan was the silver-tongued orator of the convention. By the time the proceedings ended, he was also the Democratic candidate for President.

As if the convention delegates had not repudiated Cleveland enough by ignoring his support for the gold standard, they added further insult by refusing to pass a resolution commending his administration. Bryan and his closest colleagues may have gone too far, though, for many delegates headed home with a new thought in mind — forming another political party. In fact, they did put together another political organization and asked Cleveland to run. He refused kindly, but firmly.

Problems to the End

Cleveland took no part in the campaign that followed. He was amused as William Jennings Bryan crisscrossed the nation by train and buggy, speaking hour after hour, day after day. "He'll speak in a pig pen if the pigs will listen," one of his advisors told Cleveland, which brought an agreeing nod.

On the other hand, the Republican challenger, William McKinley, stayed peacefully at home in Canton, Ohio, greeting visitors and speaking on a one-to-one basis. When the election was held in November, McKinley won by approximately half a million popular votes and a 60-40 percent victory in electoral votes. It was clear that many regular Democratic voters had crossed party lines and voted Republican, largely to protest how Cleveland had been treated by Bryan and his supporters.

Cleveland had hoped to leave office quietly, but his plans suffered a major upset. The nearby island of Cuba found itself caught up in a rebellion, with native revolutionaries trying to free the colony from its mother country, Spain. Nearly $50 million of American money was invested in Cuba, and the investors demanded that Cleveland take action to protect their endangered investments. Moreover, stories of bloody slaughter and torture by Spanish soldiers caused the American public to cry out for action. Some even suggested war against Spain, an action that Cleveland rejected. Cleveland did try to bring about a peaceful negotiation in his final months in office, but the matter finally had to be left to the incoming President.

The transfer of presidential power from Cleveland to McKinley was uniquely friendly, particularly since the transfer was from one political party to another. Cleveland had con-

Whenever he could find time, Cleveland enjoyed going on hunting and fishing expeditions. Here he is seen (seated second from left) with a group of friends on a duck-hunting trip in South Carolina. (Library of Congress.)

siderable respect for McKinley, and their unified support of a sound gold standard offered a base of agreement. Cleveland entertained his successor at dinner on the evening of March 3, 1897, then watched quietly the next day as William McKinley was sworn in as the 25th President of the United States. At 60 years of age, Grover Cleveland was totally unemployed. He smiled as he left the inauguration ceremonies, then headed to a dock on the Potomac River, where a steamer awaited to take him on a two-week fishing and hunting expedition.

Former President Grover Cleveland stands on the porch of his Princeton, New Jersey, home in 1900. (Library of Congress.)

Chapter 11
Sunset

Grover and Frances Cleveland pondered the thought of where to live after leaving the White House. Buffalo held too many sad memories for both of them. New York City had been exciting—perhaps too much so with all its hustle and bustle. No, it would not be New York City.

There was no need to practice law, for the ever-frugal Cleveland had saved one-third of a million dollars during his lifetime, a small fortune for the latter part of the 19th century. The former President also wanted no more of public life, a life where he and his family were constantly open to inspection and criticism. Soon Cleveland found the home he wanted—a two-story stone and stucco house in Princeton, New Jersey. The pace would be slower there, but with Princeton University nearby, it would not be dull.

ACADEMIC CONNECTIONS

Princeton University came to figure more and more in Cleveland's life. He enjoyed visiting the school, offering guest lectures in government and economics. Surely the students could not have found a more experienced instructor. He also

Former President Grover Cleveland sits at his desk in March of 1908. He died in Princeton, New Jersey, three months later. (Library of Congress.)

followed current affairs closely—the Spanish-American War proving to be a great frustration. To Cleveland, the United States had no right injecting itself in a matter between a colony and its mother country. "It is always a danger with imperialism," said the former President, "that a major power feels it has the right to meddle in the affairs of any other country." But as frustrating as the Spanish-American conflict was to him, the death of the free silver movement was most satisfying.

Few incidents saddened Cleveland more than the assassination of President McKinley in September of 1901. It marked the third time in Cleveland's lifetime that he had suffered through the murder of a President—Abraham Lincoln in 1865, James Garfield in 1881, and finally, McKinley. Speaking to reporters, Cleveland bemoaned the fact that "that office that holds the grandest power and responsibility shall always have death lurking nearby."

But 1901 also brought a special joy to Cleveland—he became a trustee of Princeton University. He shared a special friendship with the institution's president, Woodrow Wilson, although neither man suspected that one day Wilson would occupy the White House, too.

In 1905, Cleveland accepted a trustee position with the Equitable Life Assurance Society. The insurance company had recently undergone an investigation that had uncovered some questionable practices. Cleveland helped reorganize the company, and in 1907 became head of the Association of Presidents of Life Insurance Companies.

No greater satisfaction came to Cleveland in his later years than the joy of his wife and children. "There is no prouder father in all the country," observed one friend. The death of his first-born, Ruth, in 1904, plunged Cleveland into deep grief.

In his later years, Cleveland began experiencing many physical difficulties as a result of deteriorating kidneys and a bad heart. In his final years, while a faithful Frances Cleveland looked after him, he seldom left the house because of his poor health.

Death came to Grover Cleveland in his Princeton home on June 24, 1908. His final words were, "I have tried so hard to do right."

Chapter 12

The Cleveland Legacy

"**I** have always believed a man should be honest," observed Teddy Roosevelt, "but I'm also of the notion that a man can be too honest. Look at Grover Cleveland. His honesty got him into a kettle of hot soup. Of course, his stubbornness was a part of it too."

One would expect such a comment from Roosevelt, a Republican, about Cleveland, a Democrat. Yet there is considerably more than political jabbing in Roosevelt's words; there is also keen political sense. For in evaluating the legacy of the Cleveland presidencies, it is impossible to analyze the events of the times without some understanding of the character of Grover Cleveland himself.

A MAN FOR THE TIME

The years immediately following the Civil War represented an exciting rebirth in the United States. Rugged, untamed wilderness became fertile fields of farmland; sturdy buildings of plaster and steel sprung up within towns and cities; railroads stretched like ribbons across the breadth of the nation; businesses and industries flexed their muscles; artists created grand music and rich canvasses; writers gave new life to old words. Truly, it was an age gilded with the gifts of human effort and talent. Life was exciting in America, even exhilarating.

And yet, as Henry Adams, one of the most eloquent spokesmen of the time, put it: "No period so thoroughly ordinary has been known in American politics since Christopher Columbus first disturbed the balance of power in American society." Adams continued, "One might search the whole list of Congress, Judiciary, and Executive during the twenty-five years 1870 to 1895 and find little but damaged reputations. The period was poor in purpose and barren in results."

Historians have tended to back up Adams' charges. Many concrete examples can be cited to show that politicians during this 25-year-period paid little attention to the people, less attention to the needs of the nation, and no attention at all to the future. From city wards to the White House, politicians abused their offices, either by failing to perform acts that might have helped their constituents, or by committing acts that risked the entire framework of democracy.

Into this bleak picture stepped a blue-eyed, rotund fellow who lacked any formal education. By the time Grover Cleveland assumed the office of the presidency, he had only a minimum of political experience—perhaps more an asset than a liability. What he did possess, however, was an honest and independent character, a determination to do what was right and just, regardless of the opinion and pressure of others.

Early in his political career, Cleveland said, "A public office is a public trust," and he conducted his entire political life with that conviction. He was not blessed with creative and imaginative ideas, nor did he possess a gift for fiery oratory. He stumbled over chains of command, had little understanding of compromise, and possessed no patience for those who would use the political system for their own good.

Yet it was exactly these attributes that the political system needed and the people wanted. He was a politician for the people at a time when most politicians stood aloof. He seemed to listen when others chose to talk. Not that he fostered a benevolent father image, for he did not believe the nation should provide welfare support for its people. Cleveland was convinced that the people should support themselves, through their own resourcefulness and hard work. It could be validly argued that Cleveland's unwillingness to give federal aid to workers and farmers contributed to the length and depth of the depression during his second term in office.

Nonetheless, the legacy of the Cleveland presidencies stands firm. A political system that had wallowed in muck created by those who would reward friends and supporters with jobs was lifted onto a higher plain. Despite the countless battles he fought and lost over the tariff system, Cleveland alerted Americans to the dangers of overprotecting themselves from imported goods. He steered the country away from an imperialistic attitude that might have caused irreparable damage in the eyes of the world. And he did it by emphasizing that America must demonstrate a good conscience in whatever it does. Finally, he helped to establish a solid gold standard when casting it aside could have destroyed the economic stability of the nation.

Ironically, the combined results of his actions lost him the support of his own political party as well as much of his own personal popularity. Others would have made different choices. Not Grover Cleveland. "I shall make whatever decisions I must with as much wisdom as I possess," he said once. "No outcry from those around me will cause me to alter my course. No newspaper editorials or election will tell me whether I have decided correctly. For that, I shall listen to My Maker when He chooses to call me home."

Bibliography

Borden, Morton (editor). *America's Ten Greatest Presidents.* Chicago: Rand McNally, 1961. Vincent De Santis of Notre Dame University provided the provocative essay about Cleveland in this volume. With astute analysis, De Santis explores reasons that place Cleveland in the ranks of the nation's top chief executives.

Cleveland, Grover. *Presidential Problems.* New York: Century, 1904. This hard-to-find volume offers a look at those troubles faced by this particular President. It provides not only the facts of the situations, but insight into the mind of the man who lived through them.

Ford, Henry Jones. *The Cleveland Era.* New Haven: Yale University Press, 1921. The reader captures a unique feel for "The Gilded Age" that touched the Cleveland years in American history. While not always easy reading, there are many perceptive and penetrating views offered in this book.

Hoyt, Edwin P. *Grover Cleveland.* Chicago: Reilly and Lee, 1962. With a smooth-flowing narrative style, author Hoyt captures the dramatic life and times of a truly unique American. Cleveland was no ordinary man, and readers will relive the exciting moments that place him in a rightful position within the pages of history.

Hoyt, Edwin P. *Lost Statesmen.* Chicago: Reilly and Lee, 1961. Washington, Jefferson, Lincoln—don't look for them in this book. This volume is respectfully dedicated to a cluster of individuals who gave their time and talent only to be too soon forgotten. Cleveland is one of those who should indeed be "found" rather than lost.

Lynch, Denis Tilden. *Grover Cleveland: A Man Four-Square.* New York: Horace Liveright, 1932. The honesty and virtue of Cleveland are carefully explored in this fast-moving account of his life. Clearly, the man tried to mold his own image of the presidency to fit the needs of the nation's citizens as he saw them.

Morris, Richard B. *Great Presidential Decisions.* Philadelphia: Lippincott, 1960. The reader is given a special look at those momentous decisions that have carved the paths of history in America. One shares Cleveland's dilemmas as he struggles to choose a proper course for the nation.

Tugwell, Rexford Guy. *Grover Cleveland.* New York: Macmillan, 1968. A history professor and former government official himself, Tugwell offers an in-depth study of Cleveland. The book manages to be definitive without being stodgy, capturing the constant drama of a man whose honesty proved to be a constant obstacle.

Index

PRESIDENTS OF THE UNITED STATES

GEORGE WASHINGTON	L. Falkof	0-944483-19-4
JOHN ADAMS	R. Stefoff	0-944483-10-0
THOMAS JEFFERSON	R. Stefoff	0-944483-07-0
JAMES MADISON	B. Polikoff	0-944483-22-4
JAMES MONROE	R. Stefoff	0-944483-11-9
JOHN QUINCY ADAMS	M. Greenblatt	0-944483-21-6
ANDREW JACKSON	R. Stefoff	0-944483-08-9
MARTIN VAN BUREN	R. Ellis	0-944483-12-7
WILLIAM HENRY HARRISON	R. Stefoff	0-944483-54-2
JOHN TYLER	L. Falkof	0-944483-60-7
JAMES K. POLK	M. Greenblatt	0-944483-04-6
ZACHARY TAYLOR	D. Collins	0-944483-17-8
MILLARD FILLMORE	K. Law	0-944483-61-5
FRANKLIN PIERCE	F. Brown	0-944483-25-9
JAMES BUCHANAN	D. Collins	0-944483-62-3
ABRAHAM LINCOLN	R. Stefoff	0-944483-14-3
ANDREW JOHNSON	R. Stevens	0-944483-16-X
ULYSSES S. GRANT	L. Falkof	0-944483-02-X
RUTHERFORD B. HAYES	N. Robbins	0-944483-23-2
JAMES A. GARFIELD	F. Brown	0-944483-63-1
CHESTER A. ARTHUR	R. Stevens	0-944483-05-4
GROVER CLEVELAND	D. Collins	0-944483-01-1
BENJAMIN HARRISON	R. Stevens	0-944483-15-1
WILLIAM McKINLEY	D. Collins	0-944483-55-0
THEODORE ROOSEVELT	R. Stefoff	0-944483-09-7
WILLIAM H. TAFT	L. Falkof	0-944483-56-9
WOODROW WILSON	D. Collins	0-944483-18-6
WARREN G. HARDING	A. Canadeo	0-944483-64-X
CALVIN COOLIDGE	R. Stevens	0-944483-57-7

HERBERT C. HOOVER	B. Polikoff	0-944483-58-5
FRANKLIN D. ROOSEVELT	M. Greenblatt	0-944483-06-2
HARRY S. TRUMAN	D. Collins	0-944483-00-3
DWIGHT D. EISENHOWER	R. Ellis	0-944483-13-5
JOHN F. KENNEDY	L. Falkof	0-944483-03-8
LYNDON B. JOHNSON	L. Falkof	0-944483-20-8
RICHARD M. NIXON	R. Stefoff	0-944483-59-3
GERALD R. FORD	D. Collins	0-944483-65-8
JAMES E. CARTER	D. Richman	0-944483-24-0
RONALD W. REAGAN	N. Robbins	0-944483-66-6
GEORGE H.W. BUSH	R. Stefoff	0-944483-67-4

GARRETT EDUCATIONAL CORPORATION
130 EAST 13TH STREET
ADA, OK 74820